RAND ARROYO CENTER

Strategic Planning Tools for the Army Senior Reserve Officers' Training Corps Program

Nelson Lim, Bruce R. Orvis, Abigail Haddad, Christopher E. Maerzluft, Kenneth Kuhn, Henu Zhao, Sung-Bou Kim

Prepared for the United States Army

Approved for public release; distribution unlimited

For more information on this publication, visit www.rand.org/t/RR1501

Library of Congress Cataloging-in-Publication Data is available for this publication.
ISBN: 978-0-8330-9476-6

Published by the RAND Corporation, Santa Monica, Calif.

Preface

This report documents research conducted on a project entitled "Senior Reserve Officers' Training Corps Unit Productivity and Proposed Reinvestment of Resources." Its purpose was to provide the Army with a means to evaluate and rank the productivity of individual Senior Reserve Officers' Training Corps (ROTC) units; to use these results to identify programs to consider for expansion, downsizing, or closure; and to examine where resources garnered through such actions should be reinvested—either units at new schools or enhancements to existing units.

The report describes two strategic planning tools we created for the U.S. Army: the Senior ROTC Program Evaluation Tool (ROTC-PET) and the ROTC Selection Evaluation Tool (ROTC-SET). We designed these tools to assist the Army with its effort to improve evaluation and oversight of its Senior ROTC programs. The Army can use them to routinely assess the viability of existing programs in the near term, as well as for longer-term strategic decisions by changing the allocation of officer commissioning missions across specific colleges and universities. By combining policy objectives of the Army leadership and information on colleges, existing ROTC programs, and the areas surrounding colleges, these tools will help planners evaluate the recent and prospective performance of existing ROTC host programs and consider selection of other campuses to host new programs or participate to a greater or lesser extent in existing ones. The findings should be of interest to policymakers and researchers concerned with military manpower issues, including those who deal with evaluation of the performance of the services' ROTC programs and improving the production and diversity of officers commissioned through them.

The research reported here was sponsored by the Assistant Secretary of the Army for Manpower and Reserve Affairs; the Deputy Chief of Staff, G-1; and U.S. Army Cadet Command and was conducted within the RAND Arroyo Center's Personnel, Training, and Health Program. RAND Arroyo Center, part of the RAND Corporation, is a federally funded research and development center sponsored by the United States Army.

The Project Unique Identification Code (PUIC) for the project that produced this document is USA136616.

Executive Summary

The Reserve Officers' Training Corps (ROTC) program currently accounts for about two-thirds of Regular Army officer production. As student populations shift and resources tighten, both the productivity and location of ROTC units must be monitored to ensure that the Army attracts and commissions highly-qualified officers.

This report presents research on the development and application of two strategic planning tools. Using the Senior Reserve Officers' Training Corps Program Evaluation Tool (ROTC-PET), planners can simulate scenarios that include up to six strategic objectives and their relative priorities, as well as the degree to which current programs can expand the numbers of commissions, to evaluate existing ROTC programs. The ROTC Selection Evaluation Tool (ROTC-SET) allows users to evaluate schools not currently hosting or participating in ROTC programs, to help guide selection of new hosts or new participants in existing programs. The ROTC-SET also gives users a variety of possible objectives and constraints.

Based on our simulations, we recommend that the Army use the planning tools to help meet near-term operational, as well as longer-term strategic, goals for ROTC. For example, the ROTC-PET shows that, under the assumption that it is not possible for schools to increase their numbers of commissions, application of the 2014 Army evaluation criteria and methodology increases scholarship cost by 2.2 percent and decreases representation of racial/ethnic minorities among commissions by 2.6 percent, both undesirable outcomes. However, using the ROTC-PET to optimize scholarship cost and minority representation under the same assumption and Army evaluation criteria eliminates both of these outcomes. Planners also may assume that schools do have some ability to increase their numbers of commissions. Simulation of an alternative policy under that assumption *improved* racial/ethnic minority representation by 8.4 percent with little effect on scholarship cost, though it lowered science, technology, engineering, and mathematics (STEM) commissions by 3.5 percent. An alternative policy simulation improved representation of minorities by 8.8 percent and of STEM commissions by 4.1 percent but increased scholarship cost by 4.0 percent. The ROTC-SET can be used to identify top colleges and universities for any combination of four objectives: potential production, demographic diversity, academic quality, and efficiency. Users can view results nationally or by state and can include or exclude schools based on distance to and affiliation with current ROTC programs (both Army ROTC and ROTC programs from other services), as well as the size of the student body.

Contents

Figures

Tables

Summary

Background

The Reserve Officers' Training Corps (ROTC) program currently accounts for about two-thirds of Regular Army officer production. Given current fiscal constraints, the Army can no longer afford to maintain ROTC units that do not commission the requisite number of fully-qualified officers. As the student population has shifted and resources have tightened, there is a need to reexamine both the productivity and location of units to ensure that the Army ROTC attracts and commissions highly-qualified geographically- and demographically-diverse applicants, as well as students with majors that bring needed science, technology, engineering, and mathematics (STEM) expertise, and that it optimally represents the colleges and universities that U.S. youths attend. At the same time, the Army needs to examine where resources garnered from downsized or closed units should be reinvested into the expansion or opening of other units. These assessments will be important in near- and longer-term deliberations and decisions concerning the "reposturing" of the ROTC program.

Indeed, in 2013, the U.S. Government Accountability Office (GAO) issued a report calling for improved evaluation and oversight of ROTC programs. GAO reported that the relevant Department of Defense Instruction (DoDI 1215.08) does not contain clearly-defined performance measures "that provide a comprehensive understanding of the effectiveness and efficiency of ROTC programs, and service evaluations of ROTC program are ad hoc" (GAO, 2013, inside cover). More importantly, GAO reported that "the services have not established a systematic process to routinely evaluate ROTC program performance" (p. 21). GAO provided six recommendations for executive action. The most relevant recommendations to this report are as follows:

- Establish performance measures that are clearly defined and include cost components.
- Require routine evaluations of ROTC programs that measure progress against their strategic goals and objectives.
- Use the performance information resulting from ROTC program evaluations to assess and document the need for the existing number of units.

Consistent with the GAO recommendations and the current DoDI, the U.S. Army established the ROTC Program Review Process in 2014.

Purpose of This Report

The research described in this report provides the Army with tools to carry out the types of assessments described above; it leverages previous RAND Arroyo Center work on ROTC production and diversity. The report describes two strategic planning tools: the ROTC Program Evaluation Tool (ROTC-PET) and the ROTC Selection Evaluation Tool (ROTC-SET). These two planning tools integrate the Army's ROTC Program Review Process and enhance the Army's capabilities to accomplish GAO's recommended actions and meet both near-term and broad, longer-term strategic goals.

Our Approach

We developed the tools by combining public-use data from the U.S. Census Bureau and the Department of Education with administrative data from the Army. The tools provide performance measures for the ROTC programs and desirability measures for colleges and universities. We then applied predictive models and optimization strategies to meet strategic objectives of the Army ROTC program. Our methodology is designed to ensure that the measures used to represent strategic objectives are easy to understand, the methodology is transparent, and the programming codes are open and easy to inspect and maintain. We also worked closely with U.S. Army Cadet Command (USACC) staff during the development of the tools, so that they not only can use the tools, but can also modify and maintain them as necessary.

Planning Tools

Both the ROTC-PET and the ROTC-SET allow policy planners to explore the potential effect of different sets of strategic objectives and various environmental scenarios using information on existing ROTC programs, colleges, and the areas surrounding colleges. The ROTC-PET allows users to evaluate existing ROTC programs, including both the school that is hosting the program and the other schools that participate as feeders or affiliates. To help guide selection of schools to host new ROTC programs or to participate in existing ROTC programs, the ROTC-SET allows users to evaluate schools that do not currently host or participate in ROTC programs.

Using the ROTC-PET, planners can simulate scenarios that include up to six strategic objectives; weight the importance of each objective, including the individual measures that make up the objective; and set potential constraints in order to evaluate existing ROTC programs. For instance, planners can choose to simulate scenarios that will optimize equally for production, academic quality, demographic diversity, efficiency, cost, and quality of commissioned officers. In each simulation, planners are required to explicitly set their assumptions about the operational environment. For example, the user of the ROTC-PET needs to input how much "untapped productivity" of a host program he or she wants to assume for each simulation. This assumption deals with the level of increased commission production that is deemed feasible: a higher level of untapped productivity will lead to better expected outcomes, as the program recommends assigning more commissions to better-performing programs and reducing them at worse-performing ones. However, setting more untapped productivity than actually exists will lead to unrealistic outcomes.

The ROTC-SET also gives users a variety of possible objectives, weights, and constraints in order to select new schools for participation in ROTC or to expand affiliate programs (existing sites with cadets). The possible objectives to be optimized are related to potential production, demographic diversity, academic quality, and efficiency. Users can also choose whether to exclude (or include only) schools that are not within a set driving time of an existing ROTC program or are involved (or not involved) in the ROTC program of another service. Users can also exclude schools based on enrollment numbers and look only at results for a particular state.

Recommendations

We recommend that the Army use the planning tools to evaluate existing ROTC programs and explore new market opportunities; to keep up with changes in the college student population; to integrate the ROTC Program Review Process; to enhance its capability to accomplish GAO's recommended actions; and to help meet the Army's near-term, as well as longer-term, strategic goals for its ROTC program, the largest commissioning source for officers, including the optimal use of its resources.

Recommendation #1: The Army Should Use the Reserve Officers' Training Corps Program Evaluation Tool to Help in Routinely Evaluating Its Reserve Officers' Training Corps Programs and in Developing Near- and Longer-Term, Strategic Decisions

The ROTC-PET enhances the Army's capability to evaluate the performance of ROTC host programs and schools with cadets connected with these hosts, by allowing planners to discern the potential negative impact of underperforming programs. Based on the strategic objectives, the relative priority of these objectives, and explicitly-stated assumptions about the operational environment, the ROTC-PET also provides ways to mitigate negative effects.

In this report, we illustrate how planners can use the ROTC-PET to guide the near- and longer-term operation of the Army ROTC program. Table S.1 summarizes a few key results of several illustrative scenarios.

These results show how the ROTC-PET enhances the Army's capability for near-term operational and longer-term strategic planning and decisionmaking. In Scenario #1, when we apply the 2014 Army evaluation criteria and approach to achieve at least 5,165 commissions,

Table S.1
Key Results from Scenarios Illustrating Usage of the Reserve Officers' Training Corps Program Evaluation Tool, with Changes as Percentages

Scenario	Description	Scholarship Cost per Host	Racial/Ethnic Minority Representation Among Commissions	Percentage STEM Among Commissions
1	Apply the 2014 Army ROTC evaluation criteria and methodology + fixed historical mission allocation across brigades + 0 untapped productivity	+2.2	−2.6	+1.2
2	Army criteria + optimize scholarship cost + minority representation + fixed historical mission allocation across brigades + 0 untapped productivity	−0.3	+1.4	−0.9
3	Optimize production + minority representation + scholarship cost + vary mission allocation across brigades + 0.5 untapped productivity	+0.6	+8.4	−3.5
4	Optimize production + STEM + minority representation + scholarship cost + vary mission allocation across brigades + 0.5 untapped productivity	+4.0	+8.8	+4.1

results from the risk analysis of the ROTC-PET show that the scholarship cost will increase by 2.2 percent and racial/ethnic minority representation (i.e., all others except non-Hispanic whites) among commissions will decrease by 2.6 percent, both undesirable outcomes. In Scenario #2, we simulate a solution that produces the required number of commissions and complies with the 2014 Army evaluation criteria, while minimizing scholarship cost per school and maximizing representation of minorities among commissions. The ROTC-PET produces a solution that eliminates the increase in scholarship cost and eliminates the adverse effect on representation of minorities among commissions, increasing it by 1.4 percent instead.

In Scenario #3, we use the ROTC-PET to find a solution that is driven by three objectives (production, minority representation among commissions, and scholarship cost per host); it is allowed to vary mission allocation across brigades from the recent historical allocation and, to a degree (0.5 of a standard deviation), to increase production at individual host schools. In this simulation, the Army ROTC program *improves* racial/ethnic minority representation by 8.4 percent, while only increasing scholarship cost per host by 0.6 percent; STEM production declines, however, by 3.5 percent. In Scenario #4, we use the ROTC-PET to find a solution that is driven by four objectives (production, representation of STEM among commissions, minority representation among commissions, and scholarship cost per host) and is allowed to vary mission allocation across brigades and production at individual ROTC programs, as described for Scenario #3. The results for this simulation show that the Army ROTC program improves both racial/ethnic minority representation by 8.8 percent and STEM by 4.1 percent, though at increased scholarship cost of 4.0 percent. This is a result of the program trying to optimize on STEM production.[1] We note that the application of ROTC-PET in the more strategic manner suggested in Scenarios #3 and #4 demonstrates the tool's ability to accept alternative criteria. Scenarios #1 and #2 are tied to

[1] Using the model to optimize solely on scholarship costs, with fixed historical allocation across brigades and allowing an untapped productivity of 0.5, we can decrease scholarship costs by 3.6 percent.

more restrictive, relatively-fixed criteria like those discussed later in this report.

Recommendation #2: The Army Should Use the Reserve Officers' Training Corps Selection Evaluation Tool to Help to Find Ways to Supplement or Expand Existing Reserve Officers' Training Corps Programs to Meet Strategic Objectives of the Army Leadership and to Adapt to Changing Conditions of College Markets

The ROTC-SET is designed to help the Army find colleges and universities that are not currently hosting ROTC programs but that can provide cadets with desired characteristics based on a given set of strategic objectives. This includes both current non-host programs with cadets (expansion), as well as new schools with no current ROTC cadets (supplementation). Based on a set of strategic objectives and their relative importance, planners can generate a list of high-potential colleges and universities.

For example, in Figure S.1, we illustrate usage of the ROTC-SET. In this scenario, we use the ROTC-SET to identify the 25 colleges and universities that can most enhance the Army ROTC national posture to improve four objectives: potential production, demographic diversity, academic quality, and efficiency. The ROTC-SET produces the indicated schools as top candidates for possible expansion or supplemental sites. These findings are meant to be illustrative; the scenario optimizes across all four objectives and weights them equally, while also restricting results to those within an hour of existing ROTC programs. Scenarios intended to improve different combinations or weighting of the objectives could result in identification of a different set of colleges and universities. By using scenario data in conjunction with ArcGIS or another type of geographical software, it is possible to create maps like that in Figure S.1.

Figure S.1
The Top 25 Schools for Possible Expansion or Supplemental Sites Ranked by Desirability Score and Restricted to Schools Within One Hour of Driving Time to the Nearest Host School

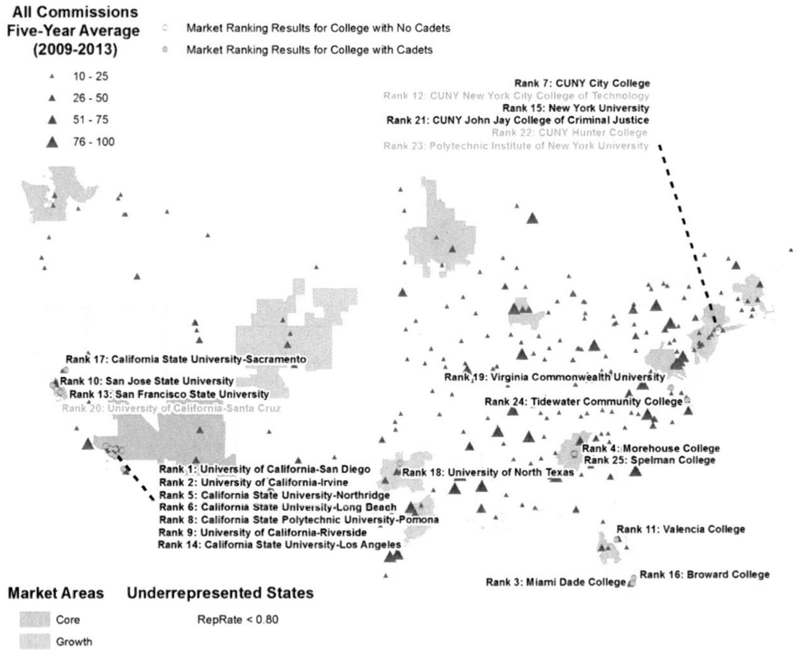

RAND *RR1501-S.1*

Acknowledgments

We would like to thank our sponsors for their critical support of the project. The expert input, access to information, and introductions to other experts provided by these individuals were integral to our research. Dr. Naomi Verdugo, Mr. Linden St. Clair, Colonel Paul Webber, Mr. Rex Harrison, Mr. Daryl Blohm, Dr. Bert Huggins, and Ms. Donna Dorminey all provided valuable information about policies and practices, as well as constructive feedback that improved our analysis at key stages of the project. We also would like to thank Mr. Kevin Thorson for providing excellent assistance to our research team at each stage of the study. We are grateful to RAND colleague Dr. Charles Goldman and Dr. Ann Parcell from CNA for their insightful reviews and thoughtful comments concerning our earlier drafts. If we have omitted any individuals or organizations that assisted us we offer our apologies and sincere gratitude for their help.

Abbreviations

ACS	American Community Survey
AIC	Akaike information criterion
BIC	Bayesian information criterion
DoD	U.S. Department of Defense
DoDI	Department of Defense Instruction
GAO	U.S. Government Accountability Office
HBCU	Historically Black College or University
HSI	Hispanic-serving institution
IPEDS	Integrated Postsecondary Education Data System
MS	Military Science
MS *x*	*x*th year of the Military Science curriculum
NDAA	National Defense Authorization Act
OLS	Ordinary Least Squares
OMS	Order of Merit Score
PET	Program Evaluation Tool
PUMS	Public Use Microdata Sample
ROTC	Reserve Officers' Training Corps

ROTC-PET	Reserve Officers' Training Corps Program Evaluation Tool
ROTC-SET	Reserve Officers' Training Corps Selection Evaluation Tool
SET	Selection Evaluation Tool
STEM	science, technology, engineering, and mathematics
USACC	U.S. Army Cadet Command

CHAPTER ONE

Introduction

Background

The Reserve Officers' Training Corps (ROTC) program currently accounts for about two-thirds of Regular Army officer production. Given current fiscal constraints, the Army can no longer afford to maintain ROTC units that do not commission the requisite number of fully-qualified officers. As the student population has shifted and resources have tightened, there is a need to reexamine both the productivity and location of units to ensure that Army ROTC attracts and commissions highly-qualified geographically- and demographically-diverse applicants and students with majors that bring needed science, technology, engineering, and mathematics (STEM) expertise and that it optimally represents the colleges and universities attended by our nation's youth. At the same time, the Army needs to examine where resources garnered from downsized or closed units should be reinvested into the expansion or opening of other units. These assessments will be important in near- and longer-term deliberations and decisions concerning the "reposturing" of the ROTC program.

Under the provisions of the National Defense Authorization Act (NDAA) for Fiscal Year 2013, Section 554 (Pub. L. 112-239, 2013), Congress mandated the U.S. Government Accountability Office (GAO) to assess the productivity, structure, and oversight of the military services' ROTC programs. In 2013, GAO issued a report calling for improved evaluation and oversight of ROTC programs. GAO reported that half of the Department of Defense's (DoD's) ROTC units did not meet the department's minimum average annual production requirement of 15 commissions per year and that cost per commissioned officer varies greatly across ROTC units (GAO, 2013, pp. 9, 15, 17). GAO also reported that the relevant DoD Instruction (DoDI 1215.08) does not provide clearly-defined performance measures "that provide a comprehensive understanding of the effectiveness and efficiency of ROTC programs" and concluded that "service evaluations of ROTC program are ad hoc" (GAO, 2013, inside cover). GAO concluded that "the services have not established a systematic process to routinely evaluate ROTC program performance" (GAO, 2013, inside cover). GAO provided six recommendations for executive action (GAO, 2013, p. 29). The recommendations most relevant to this report are as follows:

- Establish performance measures that are clearly defined and include cost components.
- Require routine evaluations of ROTC programs that measure progress against their strategic goals and objectives.
- Use the performance information resulting from ROTC program evaluations to assess and document the need for the existing number of units.

The U.S. Army Reserve Officers' Training Corps Program Review Process

In accordance with the GAO recommendations and the current DoDI, the Army established the ROTC Program Review Process in 2014 (see Secretary of the Army, 2014). The Army plans to evaluate each hosting college's and university's program annually and provide the assessment to leaders of these institutions in June of each year; the first of these evaluations took place in June 2014. The review process will determine which programs best meet Army requirements.

The Army defines five evaluation categories and criteria for host programs as follows:

1. Production:
   a. Whether the annual number of commissions produced by a host program is at least 15, at least 12 but fewer than 15, or

at least 10 but fewer than 12 commissions, based on a three-year, five-year, or ten-year average

2. Quality:
   a. Whether the commissioned officers whom a host program produced exceed the Army ROTC overall five-year average Order of Merit score (OMS) average, which indicates the Army ROTC overall ranking of each graduating cadet compared with his/her commissioning classmates on academic, physical, and military characteristics
3. Academic representation:
   a. Whether the number of commissioned officers with STEM degrees produced by a host program is greater than the five-year average for Army ROTC overall
   b. Whether a host program has a production rate of STEM-degreed graduates that exceeds the national average
   c. Whether a host program is an Historically Black College or University (HBCU) or an Hispanic-Serving Institution (HSI)
4. Geographic representation:
   a. There must be at least one public institution per state.
   b. A state's residents must be adequately represented in the Army's ROTC commissions relative to its population.
   c. Whether a host program is located in a growth or core recruiting market as determined by the U.S. Army Cadet Command (USACC)
5. Cost:
   a. Whether a host program has a retention rate of freshmen to sophomores that exceeds the USACC host institution average
   b. Whether a program's cost per commissioned officer is less than the USACC five-year average cost.

The review process determines whether a host program should be considered as a viable host or extension center. A program can be considered a viable host under any of four conditions:

- Produces at least 15 commissions per year (category "A")
- Produces at least 12 but fewer than 15 commissions and meets at least one of the criteria 3a, 4a, 4b, or 4c (category "B")
- Produces at least 10 but fewer than 12 commissions and meets at least two of the criteria 3a, 4a, 4b, or 4c (category "C")
- Is the last public host institution in a state (category "D").

If a program does not meet any of the above conditions for hosts, the Army could consider retaining the program as an extension under either of two conditions:

- It produces at least 10 commissions annually; meets the historically black or Hispanic-serving criterion; and is within one hour of driving time from a viable host (category "G").
- It produces at least 10 commissions; meets at least two of the criteria 2a, 3b, 5a, or 5b; and is within one hour of driving time from a viable host (category "H").

The programs that fail to meet the requirements to be a viable host or extension center may be placed on probation status for one year or, by exception, two years. They are categorized as follows: category "E" if average production is fewer than 10 commissions annually or category "F" if the school is not within one hour's driving time from a viable host program.

Purpose of This Report

The primary objective of this report is to present the research we carried out to develop planning tools the Army can use to improve evaluation and oversight of its Senior ROTC programs. The tools can be used routinely to assess the viability of existing programs as well as for strategic posturing to meet future challenges by changing the allocation of officer commissioning missions across specific colleges and universities. This includes evaluating the recent and prospective performance of existing ROTC host programs and considering selection of other campuses to host new ROTC programs or participate to a greater or lesser extent in existing ones.

To accomplish this objective, we developed a program evaluation framework that is consistent with the current Army evaluation criteria and an interactive tool, the ROTC Program Evaluation Tool (ROTC-PET), that improves transparency and provides a better connection to a broader set of strategic objectives. The results show that the ROTC-PET enhances the Army's capability for near-term operational and longer-term strategic planning and decisionmaking. This includes identifying and addressing possible adverse effects of applying the 2014 Army evaluation criteria and methodology under the current DoDI. The ROTC-PET also can be used to find solutions driven solely by strategic objectives rather than by the current evaluation criteria. We note that the application of ROTC-PET in that more strategic manner can be used to evaluate alternative criteria.

In addition, we developed an evaluation framework the Army can use to assess the desirability of potential expansion sites for the ROTC program in order to improve the future strategic posture of the program. In this report, we describe a spreadsheet tool, the ROTC Selection Evaluation Tool (ROTC-SET), that implements the selection evaluation framework. The ROTC-SET is designed to help the Army find colleges and universities that are not currently hosting ROTC programs but that can provide the Army with cadets with desired characteristics based on a given set of strategic objectives. This includes both current non-host programs with cadets (expansion) and new schools with no current ROTC cadets (supplementation). Based on a set of strategic objectives and their relative importance, planners can generate a list of high-potential colleges and universities.

Our Approach

As shown in Figure 1.1, we combined public-use data from the U.S. Census Bureau and the U.S. Department of Education with administrative data from the U.S. Army to develop performance measures for the ROTC programs and desirability measures for colleges and universities. We then applied predictive models and optimization strategies that meet strategic priorities of the Army ROTC program. Our aim is not to provide a set of static recommendations. Instead, we provide interactive evaluation tools that the Army can use to routinely evaluate individual ROTC programs and the strategic posture of the overall program.

Figure 1.1
Our Approach Combines Multiple Data Sources and Methodologies

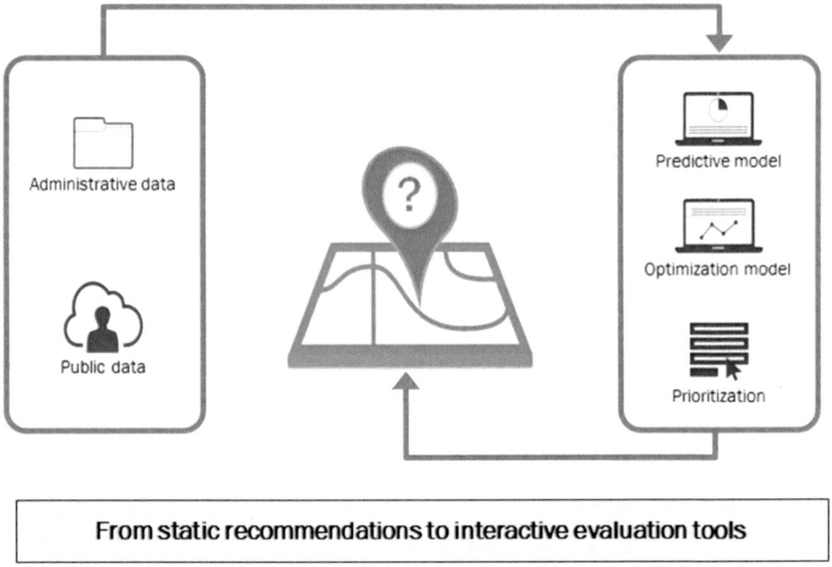

RAND *RR1501-1.1*

Organization of This Report

The report is organized as follows. In Chapter Two, we first describe an evaluation framework that provides the foundation for the ROTC-PET. We specify strategic objectives and performance measures representing these objectives and related criteria. Then, we describe the ROTC-PET user interface (UI) and optimization/prioritization algorithm that we use to develop solutions that meet the objectives and criteria. We report results from a few selected scenarios to demonstrate the usage and utility of the ROTC-PET. In Chapter Three, we describe an evaluation framework for assessing potential expansion sites that improve the strategic posture of the Army ROTC program to meet emerging trends at colleges and universities. Next, we describe the elements of the ROTC-SET: strategic objectives, performance measures, and methodology. We conclude our description of the ROTC-SET with results from illustrative scenarios. Chapter Four summarizes the key elements of the models and discusses potential policy implications of their application. We also include five appendixes. Appendix A discusses the methodology of the ROTC-PET. Appendix B reviews the data used to construct the measures in the ROTC-PET. Appendix C analogously reviews the data used to construct the measures in the ROTC-SET. Appendix D reviews the methodology to construct the measures in the ROTC-SET. Last, Appendix E presents regression results for the factors and related modeling variables used in the ROTC-SET.

CHAPTER TWO

The Reserve Officers' Training Corps Program Evaluation Tool (ROTC-PET)

We developed the ROTC-PET tool to enable users to evaluate the performance of individual ROTC programs and assess the potential effects that applying particular sets of objectives and operational assumptions can have on achievement of specific goals and key performance indicators. We designed the ROTC-PET to comply with the 2014 Army ROTC Program Review Process and criteria. Planners can simulate scenarios by applying the model to examine the potential effect of applying six "Strategic Objectives": "Production," "Academic Quality," "Demographic Diversity," "Efficiency," "Cost," and the "Quality of Commissions." And, importantly, planners can also simulate scenarios to mitigate potential negative outcomes.

In doing the evaluation, the ROTC-PET model can consider up to 11 indicators that we group into the six "Strategic Objectives." The ROTC-PET allows the user to specify the relative importance of each of the 11 indicators, as well as the desired total number of commissions; "Untapped Productivity" (the degree to which it is possible for existing ROTC programs to increase the number of commissions they produce); whether the user wants to preserve the historical proportion of commissions by brigade; and whether the user wants to evaluate ROTC programs at the host school level or the "Academic" (individual school with cadets, whether or not a host school) level.

This chapter explains each of these indicators and constraints, goes through the user interface, and presents the results from four scenarios with different goals. Each set of results consists of recommendations for how many commissions each program should target, including zero for those that it recommends be considered for possible closure. The program also displays historical metrics, such as the percentages of commissions related to demographic diversity or various costs, and how they would change under the scenario presented. Finally, the program presents a category distribution of each set of programs—those that continue to operate and those that are closed down—according to the schema that the Army developed for assessing ROTC programs. For detailed information on the methodology underlying the ROTC-PET, see Appendix A.

Six Strategic Objectives, Eleven Indicators, Other Input Parameters

This section describes the six "Strategic Objectives" represented by the 11 indicators that are used by the ROTC-PET in evaluating existing programs, as well as the other inputs planners need to determine to simulate scenarios. Table 2.1 shows each of these indicators. The data on the programs we evaluate come from the Integrated Postsecondary Education Data System (IPEDS), *U.S. News and World Reports* college

Table 2.1
Reserve Officers' Training Corps Evaluation Indicators for Individual Schools

Category	Indicator	Description
Strategic Objectives		
Production	Program Commissions	Number of commissions
	Growth	State population projections
Academic Quality	Technical Production	Percentage STEM degree academic majors
	Academic Ability	SAT 75th percentile for students
	Admission Selectivity	Percentage of applicants rejected

Table 2.1—Continued

Category	Indicator	Description
Diversity	Racial/Ethnic Diversity	Number of minority commissions (i.e., not white non-Hispanic)
	Gender Diversity	Number of female commissions
Efficiency	Proportion Commissioned	Number of commissions divided by the number of cadets
Cost	Personnel Costs	Costs of ROTC staff
	Scholarship Costs	Number of ROTC scholarships given, scaled by the school's out-of-state tuition cost
Quality of Commissions	Order of Merit Score	USACC's assessment of academic achievement and officer potential
Other Indicators		
	Desired Total Mission	Total goal for commissions nationally
	Mission Allocation Across Brigades	Fixed (keeping proportion of commissions by brigade the same as their historical averages) or variable (letting the proportion of commissions by brigade vary from historical averages)
	Untapped Productivity	In standard deviations using the annual number of commissions by school for the past five years, the amount by which schools can increase their commission output
	Evaluation Unit	Whether to evaluate schools at the host school level or the academic (all individual schools) level
	U.S. Army Current Evaluation Criteria	Whether to exclude schools that do not meet some or all of the Army's current evaluation criteria

data, and ROTC administrative data. For more comprehensive information to assist with reproducing these data or updating the data for future years, see Appendix B.

Indicators and Priority Weights

Eleven evaluation indicators are used to represent six strategic objectives. The planner chooses how to prioritize each of the indicators. The planner can indicate the relative priority of each indicator by giving it a "weight" ranging from 1 to 10. These priority weights are relative: if a planner sets one at "1" and the other at "2," the user will get the same results as if one had been set at "5" and the other at "10."

Production

Program Commissions

"Program Commissions" is the average number of annual commissions the ROTC program has produced over the past five years. These data come from the ROTC administrative dataset.

Growth

"Growth" is the projected increase in population by state and thus potential recruits.

Academic Quality

Technical Production

"Technical Production" is the percentage of enrolled students who are majoring in STEM fields. STEM majors include engineering and the physical sciences. This is from the 2012 IPEDS data. As more recent data become available, the tool can be updated to use the more recent data.

Academic Ability

"Academic Ability" refers to the 75th percentile of math SAT scores, the 75th percentile of verbal SAT scores, and the 75th percentile of writing scores among first-year, non-transfer students. This is from the 2012 IPEDS data. When those were not available, we imputed them via the 75th percentile of the composite ACT score using an SAT-to-ACT concordance table. When IPEDS was missing both SAT and ACT data, we used SAT data from the 2012 *U.S. News and World Report* college data. We were able to cover all schools in this manner. Again, the tool can be updated over time to use more recent data.

Admission Selectivity

"Admission Selectivity" is the percentage of applicants that the school accepts. This is from the 2012 IPEDS data.

Diversity

Racial/Ethnic Diversity

"Racial/Ethnic Diversity" is the average number of minority (i.e., not white non-Hispanic) commissions produced annually by the program over the past five years. These data come from the ROTC administrative dataset.

Gender Diversity

"Gender Diversity" is the average number of female commissions produced annually by the program over the past five years. These data come from the ROTC administrative dataset.

Efficiency

Proportion Commissioned

"Proportion Commissioned" is the number of commissions in the program divided by the number of cadets produced by the program over the past five years. These data come from the ROTC administrative dataset.

Cost

Personnel Costs

Each host program maintains a certain unit of service people to operate the ROTC program both at the host school and at its affiliated schools. The total cost for this contingent of staff over the past five years is defined as "Personnel Costs." These data come from the ROTC administrative dataset.

Scholarship Costs

"Scholarship Costs" are the average total amount of money spent on scholarships annually over the past five years. Our variable for this is equal to the number of scholarships a school's ROTC program gives multiplied by the cost of out-of-state tuition for that school. We picked this method because we do not have data on scholarship costs for individual cadets. The data on scholarships and commissions come from the ROTC administrative dataset; the data on tuition come from the 2012 IPEDS data. When the predicted number of commissions changes (because the ROTC-PET model recommends either expanding or contracting the school's ROTC program), scholarship costs scale accordingly, under the assumption that scholarship costs per commission will remain the same.

Quality of Commissions

Order of Merit Score

"Order of Merit Score" is measured using a range of criteria including grade point average, physical fitness, and leadership skills (Career Satisfaction Program, undated). The value for each school is the average OMS of its students within the program in the past five years. These data come from the ROTC administrative dataset.

Other Input Parameters of the Reserve Officers' Training Corps Program Evaluation Tool

The other parameters of the ROTC-PET are the following. In each case, the user specifies values for these parameters.

Desired Total Mission

The "Desired Total Mission" is the target number of total commissions nationally per year.

Mission Allocation Across Brigades

There are two options. If the user selects "Variable Allocation," the tool will disregard the historical distribution of commissions across brigades. Instead, the tool will allocate the number of commissions across brigades to achieve the best solution based on the selected "Strategic Objectives" indicators and their priority weights.

If the user selects "Historical Fixed Allocation," each brigade will be allocated the same proportion of commissions that it has historically produced. Instead of ranking all of the schools together, the model will produce separate rankings of the schools by brigade, and then will select the top schools by brigade, not overall, until the appropriate proportion has been allocated. For instance, because Brigade #1 has historically produced 11.5 percent of the ROTC commissions, regardless of the selection of "Strategic Objectives" indicators and their weights, if the planner selects "Historical Fixed Allocation" 11.5 percent of the desired mission will be allocated to Brigade #1.

Although the "Historical Fixed Allocation" option allows the tool to find a possible solution, the "Variable Allocation" option provides the planner with more flexible scenarios. Because the "Historical Fixed Allocation" option imposes a major constraint, the planner will generally make smaller improvements in terms of the "Strategic Objectives" than if the planner selected "Variable Allocation"; indeed, the planner might find it more difficult to get any solution at all, meaning that the planner will have to increase the "Untapped Productivity" parameter or decrease the "Desired Total Mission."[1]

Untapped Productivity

"Untapped Productivity" is a factor that the user has to assume to indicate how much extra production capability each ROTC program has in terms of the number of commissions it could be producing. This is quantified in terms of standard deviations using data from the past five years. For instance, if a program produced 20 commissions annually in 2009 and 2010, and 30 commissions annually in 2011–2013, it has a mean of 26 commissions per year and a standard deviation of about 5.5 commissions. If the user specifies a value of "Untapped Productivity" of "1," he/she is saying that, if asked, this school can be counted on to produce the mean + 1 standard deviation of commissions, or 26 + 5.5 = 31.5 commissions on average. The more "Untapped Productivity" the user specifies, the more ability the ROTC-PET has to improve expected outcomes for the "Strategic Objectives." This is because the ROTC-PET predicts improved outcomes by expanding the programs at the better-performing schools and shrinking or eliminating the worse-performing ones. Specifying more untapped productivity than actually exists in the system, however, will lead to

---

[1] If the mission is unattainable given "Untapped Productivity," the tool reports "WARNING: Unable to Reach Desired Mission With Set Untapped Productivity, Please Adjust Inputs." This will appear at the top of the "Program-Level Results" tab, but the program will still produce output despite not attaining the mission.

recommendations for expanding ROTC programs beyond what is realistic.

Evaluation Unit

The planner can choose to evaluate schools either at the "Host" level or at the "Academic" level. If the planner chooses to evaluate at the "Host" level, the unit that will be evaluated is the host, including all of the schools that participate in its ROTC program. This option does not allow exploration of potential organizational changes within each host program. If the planner chooses to evaluate at the "Academic" level, each individual school will be assessed for expansion or contraction, meaning that a host program can be kept open even if one or more of the schools that it currently hosts are removed from the ROTC program, and an academic unit can be kept open even if its current host is closed under the assumption that it will find another program to host it.

Army's Evaluation Criteria

As we reported earlier, the ROTC-PET is fully compliant with the 2014 Army ROTC evaluation criteria and methodology. The user can integrate these criteria into scenarios. In addition, we also explicitly compare the results each solution produces with these criteria. To accomplish this, we assigned categories (A, B, C, and D) based on how a host performed historically. The criteria are applied in succession.

1. Category A: A host will receive category A if it produces at least 15 commissions per year.
2. Category B: A host will receive category B if it produces at least 12 but fewer than 15 commissions and meets at least one criterion (described in detail in Chapter One).
3. Category C: A host will receive category C if it produces at least 10 but fewer than 12 commissions and meets at least two criteria.
4. Category D: A host will receive category D if it does not meet the conditions for categories A, B, or C but is the last public host institution in a state.

Currently, as we described earlier, USACC considers host programs that received categories A, B, C, or D as viable hosts. We refer to these categories as USACC performance categories throughout the discussion of the tool.

Methodology

We purposely used the simplest methodology we could to simulate policy scenarios, so that the user can readily explain to stakeholders how the programs' performance is measured and what the model is doing. We use indicators that are measured in natural units. Using these indicators, the ROTC-PET assigns each host or academic program (depending on the user input) a number on the basis of how well it meets the user-selected "Strategic Objectives."[2] The number is the weighted sum of the values for the program on each of the "Strategic Objectives" indicators selected by the user, with each value weighted according to the priority that the user assigned to the associated indicator. The value for the program on each indicator ranges from 0 to 1. It is calculated using the equation

$$\frac{p_i - p_{\min}}{p_{\max} - p_{\min}},$$

where p is the value for the program on the indicator, $p_{\min}$ is the worst value for any program on the indicator (e.g., lowest percentage of STEM students), and $p_{\max}$ is the best value for any program on the indicator (e.g., greatest percentage of STEM students).

The ROTC-PET then assigns the best-scoring school the maximum number of commissions it can produce based on historical data and the "Untapped Productivity" input chosen by the user. Next, it keeps going down the list of programs until all of the commissions in the "Desired Total Mission" goal have been allocated. The larger the value for "Untapped Productivity," the fewer programs will need

2 For a more technical description of the method, see Appendix A.

to be selected, and the higher-performing they will be on average in terms of meeting the "Strategic Objectives." If the user has specified "Historical Fixed Allocation," then the proportion of commissions by brigade will be kept at its historical levels, and the ranking and selection of programs will happen within each brigade to meet the brigade's commission objective rather than overall across brigades to meet the total commission objective.[3]

The Reserve Officers' Training Corps Program Evaluation Tool User Interface (UI)

Input

When the ROTC-PET runs, the user will first see the input table, shown in Figure 2.1. This is where the user does the following:

- Checks the boxes of the "Strategic Objectives" that he/she wishes for the algorithm to include
- Uses the "Priority Weights" sliders to select the relative importance of each strategic objective
- Selects an "Evaluation Unit" ("Host" or "Academic" school)
- Selects a "Mission Allocation Across Brigades" rule ("Variable" or "Historical Fixed")
- Inputs a "Desired Total Mission" number
- Inputs an "Untapped Productivity" number

[3] The procedure we use is not an optimization in a pure sense. Although the results the model recommends are based on the best historical rankings given a user's selected inputs, the increase or decrease in production at each school could alter the expected outcomes in a way that is suboptimal given those changes. For example, when scholarships are selected for optimization, the model ranks schools based on the total costs of scholarships they pay. Then, after the model determines which programs to keep and how much production changes, it calculates the new costs of scholarships by proportionally changing the dollar amounts accordingly. If a program that is inefficient with its scholarships has been selected to increase its production, the output will not be as optimal, from a scholarship perspective, as if an efficient program had been selected. In future versions, we would look to evaluate the expected output rather than the input for the factors used in meeting ROTC strategic objectives.

- If desired, selects one or more "U.S. Army Current Evaluation Criteria" to be included in the simulation. For instance, if the user selects "More than or equal to 15 commissions," all programs producing at least 15 commissions annually on average over the past five years will be considered to be performing adequately for the purpose of potential selection.

Figure 2.1
The Input Tab

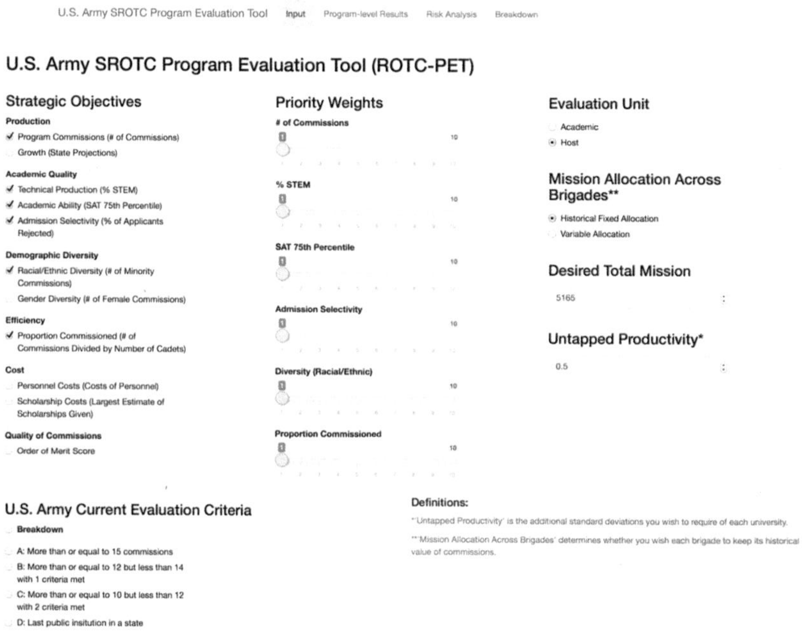

NOTE: To fit the important content on the screen, we have truncated the top lines of text, which contain the name of the program and the tabs.
RAND *RR1501-2.1*

Program-Level Results

Figure 2.2 shows the "Program-Level Results" tab. This tab shows the user how many commissions the program recommends assigning per host or academic program (again, all schools with current cadets whether a host or not) depending on which he/she selected in the "Input" tab, as well as the performance category (A, B, C, D, E, F, G, or H) from USACC in 2014 for the host schools (affiliated schools receive the category of their host) and the historical production numbers (average commissions annually over the past five years).

Figure 2.2
Program-Level Results Tab

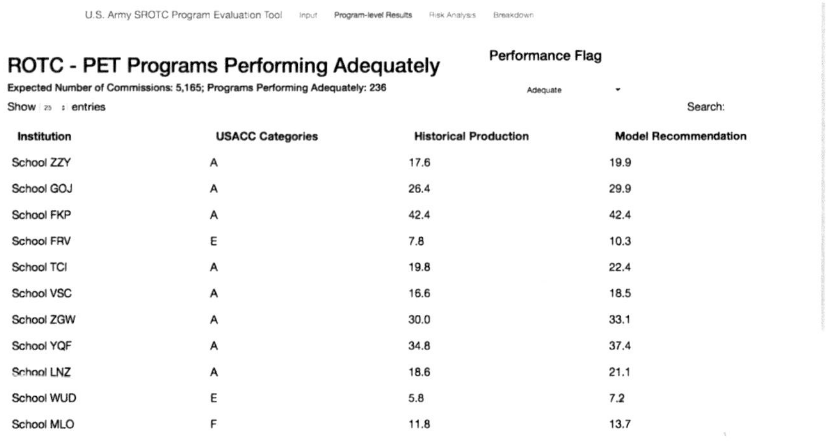
U.S. Army SROTC Program Evaluation Tool Input Program-level Results Risk Analysis Breakdown

ROTC - PET Programs Performing Adequately

Performance Flag

Expected Number of Commissions: 5,165; Programs Performing Adequately: 236

Adequate

Show 25 entries

Search:

Institution	USACC Categories	Historical Production	Model Recommendation
School ZZY	A	17.6	19.9
School GOJ	A	26.4	29.9
School FKP	A	42.4	42.4
School FRV	E	7.8	10.3
School TCI	A	19.8	22.4
School VSC	A	16.6	18.5
School ZGW	A	30.0	33.1
School YQF	A	34.8	37.4
School LNZ	A	18.6	21.1
School WUD	E	5.8	7.2
School MLO	F	11.8	13.7

RAND *RR1501-2.2*

The user can interact with the tab in the following ways:

- The "Performance Flag" box: Here, the user selects whether he/she wants to see a list of "Adequate" or "Underperforming" schools. "Adequate" schools are schools that meet the "Strategic Objectives" indicators that the user entered in the "Input" tab. Underperforming schools are schools that fail to meet those objectives.[4] "Adequate" performance means that they were ranked above the cut line of schools included to produce the "Desired Total Mission" number of commissions. As can be seen in Figure 2.2, schools above the cut line may not have received a

[4] Note that the model rates and ranks schools against the "Strategic Objectives," priorities, and parameter values that the user selects.

category of A, B, C, or D from USACC in 2014. The converse also is true; in such cases schools categorized as A, B, C, or D by USACC may be considered underperforming and below the cut line by ROTC-PET.

- The "Show _ entries" box: Here, the user selects how many records he/she wants to see per page.
- The "Search" box near the top of the figure: Here, the user can filter his/her results by not just school name, but also "USACC Categories," "Historical Production," or "Model Recommendation."
- Search boxes at the bottom of the "Program-Level Results" tab (not visible in Figure 2.2): Here, the user can filter results by searching through each column. For instance, if he/she would like to see schools with "Illinois" in their name, he/she can enter the word "Illinois" into the search box under the heading "Institution" to filter the results.
- The arrows at the top of each column: Here, the user can sort the results in ascending or descending order.

Risk Analysis Tab

Figure 2.3 shows the top part of the "Risk Analysis" tab. This shows the overall impact on "Strategic Objectives" and key performance indicators based on the scenario that the user entered on the "Input" tab. Figure 2.3 shows the results for the objectives chosen. Figure 2.4 contains other key performance indicators, including a detailed breakdown of "Demographic Diversity," "Academic Quality," and "Costs." In both tables, each row has a variable, with the historical output ("History," averaged over the past five years) and projected output ("Model"). The tables in the two figures are presented separately for the following purpose: Anything the user does with one of the tables produced in the "Risk Analysis" tab will not affect the other table. Users can interact with each table in the following ways:

- The "Show _ entries" box: Here, users select how many records they want to see per page.

- The "Search" box at the top of Figure 2.3: Here, users can filter their results by text—either words or parts of words that appear in the variable name or numbers that appear in any of the other columns.
- Search boxes at the bottom of the Risk Analysis "Strategic Objectives" table (not visible in Figure 2.3): Here, users can filter results by searching through each column. For instance, if a user would like to see variables with "tuition" in their names, he/she can type "tuition" into the search box below the first column.

Figure 2.3
First Table of the Risk Analysis Tab: Strategic Objectives

U.S. Army SROTC Program Evaluation Tool | Risk Analysis

Key Metrics

Number of Programs in Model: 236

Show entries | Search:

Strategic Objectives	History	Model	% Change
Program Commissions (# of Commissions)	19.2	21.9	13.8%
Growth (State Projections)	68,409.3	70,451.6	3.0%
Technical Production (% STEM)	14.9%	16.1%	7.6%
Academic Ability (SAT 75th Percentile)	1,776.6	1,800.9	1.4%
Admission Selectivity (% of Applicants Rejected)	35.8%	37.3%	4.2%
Racial/Ethnic Diversity (# of Minority Commissions)	2.4	2.4	-0.6%
Gender Diversity (# of Female Commissions)	3.3	3.5	3.7%
Proportion Commissioned (# of Commissions divided by Number of Cadets)	39.2%	41.0%	4.6%
Personnel Costs (Costs of Personnel)	$ 4,484.1	$ 4,592.5	2.4%
Scholarship Costs (Largest Estimate of Scholarships Given)	$456,151.5	$539,253.0	18.2%
Order of Merit Score	76.8	77.0	0.2%
Strategic Objectives	History	Model	% Change

Showing 1 to 11 of 11 entries | Previous 1 Next

RAND *RR1501-2.3*

Figure 2.4
Second Table of the Risk Analysis Tab: Key Performance Indicators

Minimum Number of Commissions From a School: 1.4

100 records per page   Search:

Other Outcomes	History	Model	% Change
Demographic Diversity			
% White	68.9%	69%	0.2%
% Black	14%	13.8%	-1.5%
% Hispanic	8%	7.9%	-1.2%
% Other Race	9.1%	9.3%	1.7%
% Female	19.4%	19.1%	-1.3%
Academic Quality			
From Tier 1	7%	7%	0%
From Schools with Lowest Acceptance Rate (top 25%)	25.3%	24.2%	-4.3%
From Public Schools	72.5%	59.3%	-18.2%
From Residential Schools	72.2%	63.4%	-12.2%
US News and World Report (peer assessment score 1-2)	1.1%	1.1%	0%
US News and World Report (peer assessment score 2-3)	77.3%	63.7%	-17.5%
US News and World Report (peer assessment score 3-4)	21.2%	21.2%	0%
US News and World Report (peer assessment score 4-5)	0.4%	0.4%	0%
Costs			
Average In-State Tuition	$14613.8	$15427.7	5.6%
Average Out-Of-State Tuition	$20914.9	$21624.3	3.4%
Average Room & Board	$8908.4	$9027.7	1.3%

RAND *RR1501-2.4*

Breakdown Tab

Figure 2.5 illustrates the "Breakdown" tab, which shows the distribution of USACC categories for both adequate and underperforming schools and lists the category for each individual school. For instance, in this scenario almost all of the adequate schools are in category A, whereas the underperforming schools have a much wider distribution of categories. Users can interact with the "Breakdown" tab by selecting "Adequate" or "Underperforming" under "Performance Flag" and the categories they wish to see under "USACC Categories."

Figure 2.5
Breakdown Tab

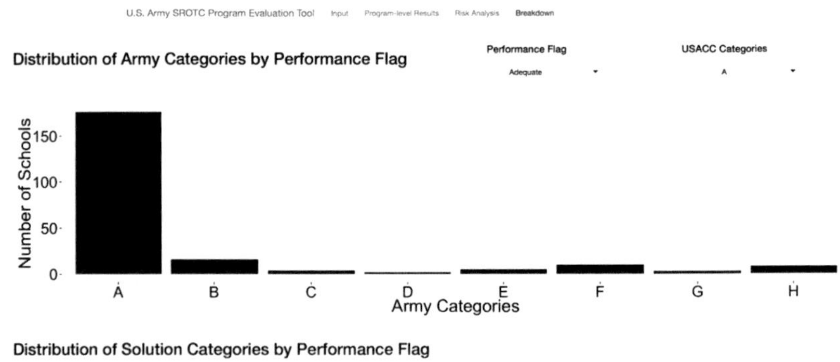

RAND *RR1501-2.5*

Illustrations of Usage of the Reserve Officers' Training Corps Program Evaluation Tool to Evaluate and Assess Reserve Officers' Training Corps Programs

In this section, we show a series of simulations that illustrate how a planner can use the ROTC-PET to conduct risk analyses and explore potential mitigation strategies to minimize potential risks.

Scenario #1: Implementation of the 2014 Army ROTC Evaluation Criteria and Methodology

In this scenario, we evaluated programs based on the 2014 Army ROTC evaluation criteria and methodology. Because we used five-year commission production averages, we did not run this scenario using the identical schools to those used by USACC (which considered several alternative commission production averages). Using the ROTC-PET, we assigned each program its historical five-year average annual number of commissions. We then accumulated commissions across the programs, starting with the top ROTC evaluation category (A) and continued down the evaluation categories until the number of commissions assigned was 5,165, with the appropriate distribution of commissions being assigned to each brigade based on keeping the historical allocation fixed. We evaluated programs at the host level.

Setup

Table 2.2 lists the settings for indicators and parameters for this scenario.

Table 2.2
Setup for Scenario #1

Inputs	Value
"Strategic Objectives" indicators	No indicator representing "Strategic Objectives" selected
Other indicators and inputs	
"U.S. Army Current Evaluation Criteria"	Selected programs based only on USACC categories until we met the desired total mission
"Desired Total Mission"	"5,165" commissions[a]
"Mission Allocation Across Brigades"	"Historical Fixed Allocation"
"Untapped Productivity"	"0" standard deviations above the historical average
"Evaluation Unit"	"Host"

[a] Without other criteria, we could not close programs in order to output only 5,165 commissions. Scenario #1 actually produces 5,176 commissions.

Program-Level Results

Given these inputs, the ROTC-PET indicates that 263 (host) programs meet the criteria and are considered to be performing adequately and that 10 (host) programs are considered to be underperforming.

Risk Analysis

The Risk Analysis tab shows the expected effect that closing the 10 underperforming programs would have on the overall Army ROTC program. In this case, the results suggest:

- Average scholarship cost per host would increase by about 2.2 percent from $456,152 to $466,351.
- Representation of racial/ethnic minorities among the commissions would decline by 2.6 percent from 29.6 percent to 28.8 percent. While overall representation among racial/ethnic minorities would decrease, the more detailed results would see some increases:[5] African Americans *decrease* by 7.1 percent, but Hispanics *increase* by 0.7 percent, and other racial/ethnic minorities *increase* by 0.9 percent.
- Even though we have selected "Historical Fixed Allocation," the brigade proportions do change a bit from historical levels because closing programs based on the Army evaluation categories does have different effects on different brigades.[6]

Breakdown

The Breakdown tab shows the distribution of USACC categories. We strictly apply the 2014 Army ROTC performance criteria within each brigade; in the end, the programs closed given a 5,165-commission goal solely have either category G or H.

---

[5] We note that, throughout the report, we generally use one digit following the decimal point in referring to percentages. The actual percentages are calculated first using the full data available and then rounded. Thus, the values reported are more accurate than those that might be calculated using only the related, rounded numbers in the tables or text.

[6] Because we are limiting the number of commissions allocated to all schools, in some cases, we can end up with a few programs that are asked to produce a small number of commissions compared to their historical production. It is assumed that these programs would be converted to affiliates or that the overall number of commissions from these programs could be spread across the host units to avoid inefficient retention and use of such host programs. This issue is more likely to appear when historical allocation is fixed.

Scenario #2: Explore Strategies to Mitigate Negative Risks Found in Scenario #1

In this scenario, we target the same number of commissions: 5,165. Our goal is to see how to mitigate two potential negative effects we found in Scenario #1: (1) rising scholarship costs and (2) declining representation of racial/ethnic minorities among the commissions. We select two "Strategic Objectives" indicators to optimize: (1) "Scholarship Costs" and (2) "Racial/Ethnic Diversity" (number of minority commissions). We set the proportion of commissions assigned to each brigade to the historical allocation and assume an "Untapped Productivity" of "0" standard deviations. The "Evaluation Unit" is "Host." Finally, we require the resulting solution to comply with the 2014 Army evaluation criteria. As is true for Scenario #1, this means that all programs getting a category of A, B, C, or D are considered before any schools not getting one of those categories are considered. However, if schools getting categories A, B, C, or D cannot meet the desired number of commissions, other schools will be included.

Setup

Table 2.3 lists the settings for indicators and parameters for this scenario.

Table 2.3
Setup for Scenario #2

Inputs	Value
"Strategic Objectives" indicators	• "Scholarship Costs" (priority weight = "1") • "Racial/Ethnic Diversity" (number of minority commissions) (priority weight = "1")
Other indicators and inputs	
"U.S. Army Current Evaluation Criteria"	Complied with the criteria. Host programs must meet the criteria to receive USACC categories A, B, C, or D in order to be considered adequate performers.
"Desired Total Mission"	"5,165" commissions
"Mission Allocation Across Brigades"	"Historical Fixed Allocation"
"Untapped Productivity"	"0" standard deviations above historical average
"Evaluation Unit"	"Host"

Program-Level Results

Given these inputs, the ROTC-PET evaluates 266 programs as adequate, while seven programs are determined to be underperforming. The model indicates that the Army can produce 5,165 commissions without those seven underperforming schools' contributions. The ROTC-PET displays historical average commissions for each host program and, alternatively, the number of commissions for the host program under the scenario. Users can compare how the solution is achieving the mission while optimizing the objectives.

Risk Analysis

The Risk Analysis tab shows the expected impact on the overall Army ROTC program if the ROTC-PET recommendations are taken. In this case, the results would change as follows:

- Scholarship cost *per host* would decrease 0.3 percent from an average of $456,152 to $454,653.

- Representation of racial/ethnic minorities among the commissions would *increase* by 1.4 percent, rather than decrease by 2.6 percent under Scenario #1: African Americans by 1.5 percent, Hispanics by 2.0 percent, and other racial/ethnic minorities by 1.1 percent.

Breakdown

The Breakdown tab shows the distribution of USACC categories. As is true in Scenario #1, there are many schools in category E, F, G, or H that are classified as performing adequately in this scenario.

Scenario #3: Solution That Optimizes Production, Racial/Ethnic Diversity, and Scholarship Cost

In this scenario, we simulate how a planner can explore ways to optimize multiple objectives *without* imposing the 2014 Army ROTC evaluation criteria. We select three "Strategic Objectives" indicators: (1) "Program Commissions," (2) "Racial/Ethnic Diversity," and (3) "Scholarship Costs."

We give equal weight (priority = "1") to all three objectives. We enter the total number of commissions as "5,165." We allow the ROTC-PET to vary the distribution of commissions across brigades from the historical allocation; in addition, we assume an "Untapped Productivity" of "0.5" standard deviations. We evaluate programs at the "Host" level.

Setup

Table 2.4 lists the settings for indicators and parameters for this scenario.

Table 2.4
Setup for Scenario #3

Inputs	Value
"Strategic Objectives" indicators	• Program commissions (number of commissions) (priority weight = "1") • Racial/ethnic diversity (priority weight = "1") • Scholarship costs (priority weight = "1")
Other indicators and inputs	
"U.S. Army Current Evaluation Criteria"	The solution does not need to comply with the 2014 Army evaluation criteria.
"Desired Total Mission"	"5,165" commissions
"Mission Allocation Across Brigades"	"Variable Allocation"
"Untapped Productivity"	"0.5" standard deviation above historical average
"Evaluation Unit"	"Host"

Given these inputs, the ROTC-PET indicates that there are 238 (host) programs that would be considered to be performing adequately and 35 (host) programs that would be considered as underperformers.

Risk Analysis

The Risk Analysis tab shows the expected impact on the overall Army ROTC program if the 35 underperforming programs are closed. In this case, the results suggest:

- Average number of commissions per host would increase by 12.3 percent from 19.3 to 21.7.
- Percentage of STEM commissions would decline by 3.5 percent from 15.8 percent to 15.2 percent.
- Average scholarship cost *per host* would increase by 0.6 percent from $456,152 to $459,111.
- Representation of racial/ethnic minorities among the commissions would increase by 8.4 percent: African Americans by 11.4 percent,

Hispanics by 9.2 percent, and other racial/ethnic minorities by 3.9 percent.

To achieve these results, the ROTC-PET suggests that the mission allocation among brigades should be changed as described in Table 2.5. For example, the ROTC-PET recommends that the mission allocation for Brigade #2 and Brigade #7 be reduced by 32.9 percent and 8.4 percent, respectively, while Brigades #1, #3, #4, #5, #6, and #8 should get additional missions of 3.8, 5.5, 3.3, 14.3, 10.7, and 5.1 percent, respectively.

Table 2.5
Historical and Scenario #3 Mission Allocation Across Brigades, as Percentages

Brigade	Historical	Recommended	Change
1	11.4	11.8	3.8
2	13.5	9.1	–32.9
3	12.8	13.5	5.5
4	12.3	12.7	3.3
5	13.4	15.3	14.3
6	13.6	15.0	10.7
7	12.2	11.1	–8.4
8	10.9	11.4	5.1
Total	100	100	

Scenario #4: Solution That Optimizes Production, STEM, Racial/Ethnic Diversity, and Scholarship Cost

In this scenario, we select four "Strategic Objectives" indicators: (1) "Program Commissions," (2) "Technical Production," (3) "Racial/Ethnic Diversity," and (4) "Scholarship Costs."

We give equal priority (weight = "1") to all objectives. We enter the total number of commissions as "5,165." We allow the ROTC-PET to vary the distribution of commissions among brigades from the historical allocation; in addition, we assume an untapped productivity of "0.5" standard deviations. We evaluate programs at the "Host" level.

Setup

Table 2.6 lists the settings for indicators and parameters for this scenario.

Table 2.6
Setup for Scenario #4

Inputs	Value
"Strategic Objectives" indicators	• "Program Commissions" (priority weight = "1") • "Technical Production" (percentage of STEM commissions) (priority weight = "1") • "Racial/Ethnic Diversity" (priority weight = "1") • "Scholarship Costs" (priority weight = "1")
Other indicators and inputs	
"U.S. Army Current Evaluation Criteria"	The solution does not need to comply with the 2014 Army evaluation criteria.
"Desired Total Mission"	"5,165" commissions
"Mission Allocation Across Brigades"	"Variable Allocation"
"Untapped Productivity"	"0.5" standard deviation above historical average
"Evaluation Unit"	"Host"

Program-Level Results

Given these inputs, the ROTC-PET indicates that there are 237 (host) programs that are considered to be performing adequately, and 36 (host) programs considered to be underperforming.

Risk Analysis

The Risk Analysis tab shows the expected impact on the overall Army ROTC program if the 36 underperforming programs are closed. In this case, the results suggest:

- Average number of commissions would increase by 12.7 percent from 19.3 to 21.8.
- Percentage of STEM commissions would increase by 4.1 percent from 15.8 percent to 16.4 percent.
- Average scholarship cost *per host* would increase by 4.0 percent from $456,152 to $474,299.
- Representation of minorities among the commissions would increase by 8.8 percent: African Americans by 11.8 percent, Hispanics by 8.9 percent, and other racial/ethnic minorities by 5.1 percent.

To achieve these results, the ROTC-PET suggests that the mission allocation among brigades should be changed as described in Table 2.7. For example, ROTC-PET recommends that the mission allocation for Brigades #2 and #7 be reduced 15.6 and 22.1 percent, respectively, while Brigades #1, #3, #4, #5, #6, and #8 should get additional missions of 3.8, 4.5, 3.8, 14.3, 8.8, and 1.9 percent, respectively.

Table 2.7
Historical and Scenario #4 Mission Allocation Across Brigades, as Percentages

Brigade	Historical	Recommended	Change
1	11.4	11.8	3.8
2	13.5	9.1	–15.6
3	12.8	13.5	4.5
4	12.3	12.7	3.8
5	13.4	15.3	14.3
6	13.6	15.0	8.8
7	12.2	11.1	–22.1
8	10.9	11.4	1.9
Total	100	100	

Conclusion

The ROTC-PET allows planners flexibility in prioritizing different indicators and instituting different constraints when evaluating existing ROTC programs. There are 11 possible "Strategic Objectives" "Indicator" variables that planners can select and prioritize. Planners also must set the number of commissions desired and the amount of "Untapped Productivity" to assume for existing ROTC programs. They also specify whether they want to evaluate schools at the host level or the academic program level, and whether the proportion of commissions by brigade can vary from historical levels. Users of the ROTC-PET can also specify whether or not they want the solution to comply with the 2014 Army ROTC evaluation criteria. The more difficult the constraints the user enters—fixing the number of commissions by brigade, entering a low number for untapped productivity or a high number for total commissions, or excluding schools that do not meet USACC standards—the less influential the actual "Strategic Objectives" will be in terms of which programs are considered to be performing adequately and which are expanded. This is because the program will not have as much room to pursue the best options for meeting the "Strategic Objectives." In addition to applying the ROTC-PET to evaluate the host programs, users also can use it to explore ways to minimize potential negative effects of attempting to meet specific goals.

CHAPTER THREE

The Reserve Officers' Training Corps Selection Evaluation Tool (ROTC-SET)

We developed the ROTC Selection Evaluation Tool (ROTC-SET) to enable users to assess the potential of schools that do not currently host ROTC programs and make recommendations regarding expansion or supplementation. The ROTC-SET is a spreadsheet that users can access via a DVD. In doing the evaluation, the ROTC-SET model considers 13 "Indicator" variables, which we have grouped into four "Strategic Objectives": "Potential Production," "Demographic Diversity," "Academic Quality," and "Efficiency." The ROTC-SET allows users to specify the relative importance of each of the 13 indicators, as well as whether they wish to impose any of several constraints. The constraints include driving time from existing ROTC programs, state, Army ROTC affiliation (whether or not they currently affiliate with an Army ROTC program), Air Force and Navy ROTC affiliation, and number of students enrolled. Based on the strategic objectives and hard constraints, the ROTC-SET produces a ranked list of schools. This chapter explains each of the indicators and presents the results from several possible scenarios involving different indicators and constraints. In all cases, the indicators are normalized into standard deviations to quantify them in the same unit of measurement. Additionally, when we refer to "students," we mean full-time students seeking degrees or certificates.

Evaluation Framework

This section describes the 13 indicators that the ROTC-SET uses in ranking potential schools, as well as the optional constraints that users can impose involving distance to existing ROTC programs, state, ROTC affiliation, and enrollment size. Table 3.1 shows each of the indicators and the "Strategic Objectives" category of which it is a part.

Table 3.1
Reserve Officers' Training Corps Selection Evaluation Tool Indicator Variables

Category	Indicator	Description
"Strategic Objectives"		
"Potential Production"	"Propensity"	Predicted number of students with some interest in ROTC
	"Commissions"	Probability that the school would produce at least 15 commissions
	"Potential Productivity"	Predicted number of MS 3 contracts at the school
	"Market Potential"	Deviation between actual and expected numbers of MS 3 contracts in a county
	"Future Enrollment"	Expected number of students at the school in 2020
"Demographic Diversity"	"Magnitude"	Number of minority students at the school
	"Representation"	Percentage of students at the school who are minorities
	"Diversity Index"	Overall measure of exposure to different racial/ethnic groups
"Academic Quality"	"Selectivity"	Acceptance rate
	"Reputation"	*U.S. News and World Report*'s peer ranking
	"STEM"	Percentage of students who are STEM majors
"Efficiency"	"Retention Score"	Predicted commission rate of cadets
	"Community Support Score"	Number of veterans living within one hour's driving time of the school

Table 3.1—Continued

Category	Indicator	Description
"Constraints" (optional)		
	Distance	"Minimum Distance" and "Maximum Distance" to the closest ROTC host program, in minutes of driving time
	"State"	All states or any individual state
	"Army ROTC Affiliation"	Only affiliates, only non-affiliates, or both affiliates and non-affiliates
	"Air Force ROTC Status"	Only affiliates or hosts; only non-affiliates and non-hosts; or both affiliates and hosts as well as non-affiliates and non-hosts
	"Navy ROTC Status"	Only affiliates or hosts; only non-affiliates and non-hosts; or both affiliates and hosts as well as non-affiliates and non-hosts
	"Minimum Enrollment"	Only schools with at least the specified number of students
	"Maximum Enrollment"	Only schools with no more than the specified number of students

NOTE: MS = Military Science. MS 3 = third year of the MS curriculum.

The data on the schools we evaluate and the areas in which they are located come from IPEDS, *U.S. News and World Report* college data, and the American Community Survey (ACS). We supplement this information with data from USACC's annual on-campus survey and with ROTC administrative data. We do so to enable us to model some of the "Potential Production" indicators for schools that currently have ROTC programs, so that we can predict these indicators for schools that do not currently have ROTC programs. For more comprehensive information to assist with reproducing these data or updating the data for future years, see Appendix C.

Potential Production

"Potential Production" consists of five different indicators. Each of these indicators is the result from a statistical model.

Propensity

"Propensity" is the predicted number of students with some interest in ROTC. We obtained the actual number of students with some interest in ROTC for schools with ROTC programs; it is based on information from a sample of undergraduates collected by USACC during the 2000s in its on-campus surveys. We then modeled this value at those schools using a logistic regression[1] with a variety of geographic area and school-level characteristics, including region, percentage of adults with college degrees, military recruit rate, number of veterans per 1,000 state population, state unemployment rate, median household income, the proportion of African American students, the proportion of Hispanic students, the proportion of male students, total yearly expense (tuition plus room and board cost), total yearly expense squared, and an index of racial/ethnic diversity which would be maximized if each racial/ethnic group were present in equal numbers. The variables are from 2012 IPEDS data and 2012 ACS data. We then used that equation and the actual area and school-level characteristics for the schools we are evaluating in the ROTC-SET to estimate the *proportion* of students with some interest in ROTC for each school in our database. We then multiplied the estimated proportion of students with some interest in ROTC by the school's total enrollment to estimate the *number* of students with some interest in ROTC.

Commissions

The "Commissions" "Indicator" variable is the probability that a school would produce at least 15 commissions annually.[2] Among schools that currently have ROTC programs, we applied a logistic regression to model whether they produced at least 15 commissions as a function of total enrollment, total enrollment squared, total yearly expense (tuition plus room and board cost), total yearly expense squared, the difficulty of gaining admission, graduation rate, percentage of full-time faculty,

---

1 In Appendix D, we discuss the regression models used to construct several of the "Indicator" variables in the ROTC-SET, and in Appendix E we show the regression results for these models.

2 The cutoff is consistent with DoDI 1215.08 and Army ROTC evaluation criteria used to consider a host viable.

the percentage of male students, state median household income, the percentage of military members in the state population, and the percentage of veterans in the school's county living within one-hour driving distance. The variables are from 2012 IPEDS data and data gathered by ROTC programs in the 2000s. We then used the resulting logistic regression equation and the actual school-level characteristics for the schools we are evaluating in the ROTC-SET to estimate the probability that each school would produce at least 15 commissions.

Potential Productivity

"Potential Productivity" is the predicted number of MS 3 contracts at a school—cadets who have signed contracts by their junior year to commission after completing college. We obtained the actual number of MS 3 contracts for schools with ROTC programs. We modeled this value at those schools using a hurdle regression with a variety of area- and school-level characteristics including region, whether the school is primarily residential, whether the school is public, the difficulty of gaining admission, graduation rate, percentage of full-time faculty, the percentage of instructors with doctorate or terminal degrees, percentage of students in physical science and engineering majors, proportion of male students, proportion of African American students, proportion of Hispanic students, the log of total enrollment, log of total yearly expense (tuition plus room and board costs), a measure of diversity that would be maximized if each racial/ethnic group were present in equal numbers, state appropriations per postsecondary student, SAT/ACT 75th percentile score at the school, state median household income, the percentage of adults in the state with college degrees, percentage of veterans within one hour driving distance, and the percentage of military members in the state's population. The variables are from 2012 IPEDS data, 2012 ACS data, and data gathered by ROTC programs in the 2000s. We then use the resulting regression equation and the actual area and school-level characteristics for the schools we are evaluating in the ROTC-SET to impute potential productivity values.

Market Potential

"Market Potential" is the deviation between the actual and expected number of MS 3 contracts in the county where a school is located. We derive this measure using the "Potential Productivity" variable. It is derived for each county by summing the predicted number of contracts in each program in the county according to the ROTC-SET model and subtracting the actual contracts observed in the county. We use the same variables as in the ROTC-PET model described in Chapter Two; they include 2012 IPEDS data, 2012 ACS data, 2012 *U.S. News and World Report* data, and data gathered by ROTC programs during the 2000s.

Future Enrollment

"Future Enrollment" is the expected number of students at a school in 2020. This is based on extrapolating the results of an Ordinary Least Squares (OLS) regression for each school[3] of its enrollment by year from 1987 to 2012: we assume that whatever trend is present over the course of that period will continue until 2020. The enrollment variable is from 1987–2012 IPEDS data.

Demographic Diversity

"Demographic Diversity" consists of three indicators relating to the demographics of students. Each of these indicators represents the normalized values of actual school-level variables from the schools being evaluated for ROTC expansion.

Magnitude

"Magnitude" is the number of minority students enrolled in the school. This is from 2012 IPEDS data. Minority students are defined as students with races or ethnicities other than "non-Hispanic white."

Representation

"Representation" is the percentage of minority students at a school. This is from 2012 IPEDS data. Again, minority students are defined as students with races or ethnicities other than "non-Hispanic white."

---

[3] We fit the OLS regression for each school, so it is not possible to present the regression results in a table.

Diversity Index

The "Diversity Index" is a variable that is maximized when all possible racial/ethnic groups are present and the same size and minimized when there is only one racial/ethnic group that accounts for 100 percent of the student population. This index was calculated from 2012 IPEDS data. Again, minority students are defined as students with races or ethnicities other than non-Hispanic white. See Appendix C for more information.

Academic Quality

"Academic Quality" consists of three indicators relating to school academics. Each of these indicators represents the normalized values of actual school-level variables from the schools being evaluated for ROTC expansion.

Selectivity

"Selectivity" is the percentage of applicants that the school accepts. This is from 2012 IPEDS data.

Reputation

"Reputation" is the peer-ranking component of *U.S. News and World Report* (here, taken from the 2012 report). The peer-ranking score is a rating of the academic quality of the school's undergraduate program by top college administrators from other schools.

STEM

"STEM" is the percentage of enrolled students who are majoring in STEM fields. This is from 2012 IPEDS data. IPEDS STEM majors include engineering and the physical sciences.

Efficiency

"Efficiency" consists of two indicators relating to efficiency. The first is based on the result of a statistical model, while the second is the normalized value of a county-level variable for the schools being evaluated for ROTC expansion.

Retention Score

"Retention Score" is the predicted retention rate of cadets. We created a variable indicating whether a cadet remained in the ROTC program from individual-level data of cadets for schools with ROTC programs. We considered that a cadet was retained if he/she commissioned. We used a logistic regression to model the probability that a cadet was retained in the ROTC program at his/her school based on area and school-level characteristics, including log of total enrollment, log of total yearly expense, school quality (i.e., whether the school is public or private, whether it is residential or nonresidential), its SAT/ACT 75th percentile score, acceptance rate, the state's postsecondary education appropriations, percentage of full-time faculty, percentage of instructors with doctorate or terminal degrees, percentage of African American and Hispanic students, percentage of male students, percentage of adults with college degrees, the state's military recruit rate, state unemployment rate, percentage of state population of veterans within one-hour driving distance, and the proportion of the state's population who are military members. Individual characteristics used in the regression include type of scholarship, MS level, and year of enrollment. The variables are from 2012 IPEDS data, 2012 ACS data, and USACC administrative data for cadets who were in an ROTC program during the 2000s. We use the resulting regression equation and the actual area and school-level characteristics for the schools we are evaluating in the ROTC-SET to predict a retention score. Because the colleges being assessed have few if any cadets, for individual characteristics we calculated across ROTC programs and applied the mean values for the schools.

Community Support Score

"Community Support Score" is the number of veterans living within one hour's driving time of the school.

Optional Constraints

We have included various constraints that are not part of the optimization process but instead act as filters, with all schools that do not meet these constraints being left out entirely. If many schools are disqualified, fewer than 25 schools could appear in the results. These filters include driving distance to nearby Army ROTC programs, state, ROTC affiliation status of the school for both the Army and other services, and number of students enrolled.

Minimum Distance and Maximum Distance

Distance in minutes is the driving time between the school being considered and the closest existing ROTC host program based on driving distance, types of roads, speed limits, and other information. The user can set minimum and maximum times, in number of minutes. For instance, the user can exclude all schools not within an hour of an existing ROTC program. This is based on current ROTC data concerning which schools have ROTC host programs and 2012 IPEDS data on where each school is located. The distances between schools we evaluated and the closest ROTC program were between 0.11 miles and 59.5 miles for schools that had ROTC programs and were within an hour's time; the average was 18.9 miles.

State

"State" is the state in which the school being considered is located. The default is that "All States" is selected, but users can select an individual state and only see schools from that state.

Army ROTC Affiliation

"Army ROTC Affiliation" describes whether each school is currently an ROTC affiliate: users can choose to see only ROTC affiliates, only ROTC non-affiliates, or both. (Schools that currently host ROTC programs are excluded regardless of what the user selects.)

Air Force ROTC Status

"Air Force ROTC Status" describes whether the school participates in Air Force ROTC, with participation including both hosting and affiliating. Users can choose to see only Air Force ROTC participants, only schools that are not involved in Air Force ROTC, or both.

Navy ROTC Status

"Navy ROTC Status" describes whether the school participates in Navy ROTC, with participation including both hosting and affiliating.

Users can choose to see only Navy ROTC participants, only schools that are not involved in Navy ROTC, or both.

Minimum Enrollment

"Minimum Enrollment" is the smallest school, in terms of the number of degree-seeking, full-time students that will be included in the results.

Maximum Enrollment

"Maximum Enrollment" is the largest school, in terms of the number of degree-seeking, full-time students, that will be included in the results.

The Reserve Officers' Training Corps Selection Evaluation Tool User Interface

The ROTC-SET is an interactive Excel spreadsheet that is bundled with the ROTC-PET on a DVD. This section discusses the user interface. The next section explores several possible scenarios using the ROTC-SET.

Instructions

The first tab of the ROTC-SET consists of instructions for the user. These are as follows (see also Figure 3.1).

1. First, go to the "User Inputs" tab and specify weights for your "Strategic Objectives." You can input any integer from "0" to "10." A value of 0 means that the ROTC-SET will not incorporate the variable at all. These weights are relative: if you enter "1" for all of them, this is the same as entering "10" for all of them.
2. Next, input values for the optional constraints.
   a. For "Minimum Distance" and "Maximum Distance," you can enter in integer numbers for the minimum and maximum driving times. The minimum must be at least 0 and the maximum must be greater than the minimum. For instance, if you enter "5" for the minimum value and "20" for the maximum value, your results will all be between 5

and 20 minutes' driving distance of the nearest ROTC host program. You must enter numbers for both distances. Any distance greater than 1,100 for the maximum value will have no exclusion effect on the results because no schools without ROTC host programs are farther than 1,100 minutes from the nearest ROTC host program.

b. For "State," you can select "All States" or select only one state.

c. For "Army ROTC Affiliation," you can select "Affiliate," which will return only schools that currently partner with ROTC host schools; "No," which will return only schools that do not partner with ROTC host schools; or "Both," which will return both.

d. For "Air Force ROTC Status," you can select "Affiliate or Host," which will return only Air Force ROTC host or affiliate schools; "No," which will return only schools that do not host or partner with Air Force ROTC host schools; or "Both," which will return all schools. (The same applies for "Navy ROTC Status.")

e. For "Size," you can enter in integer numbers for the "Minimum Enrollment" and "Maximum Enrollment" of students. The minimum must be at least 0, and the maximum must be greater than the minimum.

3. When you are finished, press "Ctrl-A" to update the results.
4. Go to the "Final Output" tab to see the top 25 schools according to the criteria you have selected. (If your constraints leave fewer than 25 schools, you will see only those schools.)

Figure 3.1
The Reserve Officers' Training Corps Selection Evaluation Tool Instructions Tab

ROTC-SET Instructions

RAND developed the ROTC Selection Evaluation Tool (ROTC-SET) to enable users to assess the potential of schools that don't currently host ROTC programs and make recommendations regarding expansion. The ROTC-SET model considers up to thirteen indicator variables which we've grouped into four strategic objectives: potential production, demographic diversity, academic quality, and efficiency. ROTC-SET allows you to specify the relative importance of each of these thirteen indicators, as well as whether you wish to impose a final "hard" constraint of maximum driving time from existing ROTC programs, in order to produce a list of the 25 best candidates for ROTC expansion.

1. First, go to the "User Inputs" tab and specify weights for your strategic objectives. You can input any integer from 0-10. A value of "0" means the ROTC-SET won't incorporate the variable at all. These weights are relative: if you enter "1" for all of them, this is the same as entering "10" for all of them.

2. Next, input values for the optional constraints.

For minimum and maximum distances, you can enter in integer numbers for the minimum and maximum. The minimum must be at least 0 and the maximum must be greater than the minimum. For instance, if you enter "5" for the minimum value and "20" for the maximum value, your results will all be between 5 and 20 minutes driving distance of the nearest ROTC program. You must enter numbers for both of these, but if you enter 0 for the minimum value and anything greater than 1,100 for the maximum value, they will have no effect on results because no schools without ROTC programs are further than 1,100 minutes from the nearest ROTC program.

For State, you can select "All States" or select only one state.

For "Army ROTC Affiliation," you can select "Affiliate," which will return only schools which currently partner with ROTC host schools, "No," which will return only schools which don't partner with ROTC host schools, or "Both," which will return both.

For "Air Force ROTC Affiliation," you can select "Affiliate or Host," which will return only Air Force ROTC host or affiliate schools, "No," which will return only schools which don't host or partner with Air Force ROTC host schools, or "Both," which return all schools. (The same applies for "Navy ROTC Affiliation.")

For "Size," you can enter in integer numbers for the minimum and maximum. The minimum must be at least 0 and the maximum must be greater than the minimum.

3. When you're finished, press "Ctrl-A" to update the results.

4. Go to the "Final Output" tab to see the top 25 schools according to the criteria you've selected. (If your constraints leave fewer than 25 schools, you'll see only those schools.)

RAND *RR1501-3.1*

User Inputs

The second tab of the ROTC-SET consists of user inputs, as illustrated and discussed below in Figure 3.2 under Setup for Scenario #1. This is where the planner uses the dropdown menu to select which "Strategic Objectives" he/she wants to use and values for the "Optional Constraints." For the "Strategic Objectives," a value of 0 means that the ROTC-SET will not incorporate the objective for the solution. For the "Optional Constraints," a value must be input. However, the user can enter a very large number for "Maximum Distance" and select "All States" and "Both" for "ROTC Program" if he/she does not want to exclude any schools from the calculation. After finishing, the user needs to press "Ctrl-A" for the program to calculate results.

Scenario #1: Using All Strategic Objectives, Looking for Schools Within an Hour of Existing Programs

In this scenario, we do not prioritize any particular strategic objective, but just look in general for high-potential schools within an hour of existing ROTC host programs.

Setup

For setup, we prioritize each of the "Strategic Objectives" "Indicator" variables at "1." For the "Optional Constraints" "Indicator" variables, we enter "0" for "Minimum Distance," and enter "60" for "Maximum Distance." This includes in our results only schools that are within an hour's driving time of existing ROTC host programs. We include "All States," select "Both" for all of the ROTC variables to include schools that are affiliated with ROTC programs and schools that are not, and input "500" and "100,000"[4] (or some other extremely-large value) for "Minimum Enrollment" and "Maximum Enrollment." Figure 3.2 shows these settings selected as the "Input Parameters."

Final Output

Figure 3.3 shows the top part of the final "Output" tab, which contains the top schools based on the user's input. They are ranked in order of desirability score, with a maximum of 25 schools showing, but fewer if the user's constraints leave less than 25 schools available. This tab also shows the nearest school that hosts an ROTC program and how far away it is in minutes, as well as what state the school is in. The "ROTC Affiliate" column contains "Yes" if the school partners with an ROTC host school and "No" if it does not, while Air Force and Navy ROTC columns show whether the school is a host, affiliate, or neither ("No"). Finally, the "Enrollment" column shows the number of students at the school. The final output shown in Figure 3.3 is based on the user inputs in Figure 3.2 for Scenario #1.

---

[4] Very few ROTC affiliate schools have fewer than 500 students. The value of 100,000 is not binding: all schools have fewer than 100,000 students. We use these constraints in all of the scenarios, although users might wish to use different ones.

Figure 3.2
Input Parameters for Scenario #1

Strategic Objectives	Indicator	Weight
Potential Production	Propensity	1
	Commissions	1
	Potential Productivity	1
	Market Potential	1
	Future Enrollment	1
Demographic Diversity	Magnitude	1
	Representation	1
	Diversity Index	1
Academic Quality	Selectivity	1
	Reputation	1
	STEM	1
Efficiency	Retention Score	1
	Community Support Score	1

Optional Constraints	Indicator	Value
Location	Minimum Distance (in minutes)	0
	Maximum Distance (in minutes)	60
	State	All States
ROTC Program	Army ROTC Affiliation	Both
	Air Force ROTC Status	Both
	Navy ROTC Status	Both
Size	Minimum Enrollment	500
	Maximum Enrollment	100,000

After you are finished entering your weights, press Ctrl-A to update the output.

RAND *RR1501-3.2*

Figure 3.3
Output from the Reserve Officers' Training Corps Selection Evaluation Tool for Scenario #1

Top 25 Schools for Possible Expansion Ranked by Desirability Score

Rank	School	Nearest Host School	Distance (minutes)	State	ROTC Affiliate	Air Force ROTC	Navy ROTC	Enrollment
1	University of California-San Diego	San Diego State University	23	CA	Yes	Affiliate	Affiliate	21,969
2	University of California-Irvine	California State University-Fullerton	27	CA	Yes	No	No	21,876
3	Miami Dade College	Florida International University	18	FL	Yes	Affiliate	No	25,750
4	Morehouse College	Georgia State University	5	GA	Yes	Affiliate	Affiliate	2,220
5	California State University-Northridge	University of California-Los Angeles	23	CA	Yes	No	No	25,536
6	California State University-Long Beach	California State University-Fullerton	27	CA	Yes	No	No	25,810
7	CUNY City College	Fordham University	9	NY	Yes	No	No	9,421
8	California State Polytechnic University-Pomona	Claremont McKenna College	15	CA	Yes	No	No	17,816
9	University of California-Riverside	Claremont McKenna College	31	CA	Yes	No	No	18,052
10	San Jose State University	Santa Clara University	9	CA	Yes	Host	No	20,271
11	Valencia College	University of Central Florida	19	FL	Yes	No	No	15,749
12	CUNY New York City College of Technology	St. John's University-New York	14	NY	No	No	No	9,945
13	San Francisco State University	University of San Francisco	9	CA	Yes	No	No	22,218
14	California State University-Los Angeles	University of Southern California	11	CA	Yes	No	No	14,979
15	New York University	St. John's University-New York	16	NY	Yes	Affiliate	No	20,950
16	Broward College	Florida International University	40	FL	Yes	Affiliate	No	12,100
17	California State University-Sacramento	University of California-Davis	24	CA	Yes	Host	No	20,603
18	University of North Texas	Texas Christian University	41	TX	Yes	Host	No	23,870
19	Virginia Commonwealth University	University of Richmond	12	VA	Yes	No	No	19,511
20	University of California-Santa Cruz	Santa Clara University	52	CA	No	No	No	15,562
21	CUNY John Jay College of Criminal Justice	Fordham University	12	NY	Yes	No	No	10,269
22	CUNY Hunter College	Fordham University	13	NY	No	No	No	11,910
23	Polytechnic Institute of New York University	St. John's University-New York	14	NY	No	No	No	1,927
24	Tidewater Community College	Norfolk State University	3	VA	Yes	No	No	11,563
25	Spelman College	Georgia State University	3	GA	Yes	Affiliate	Affiliate	2,074

RAND *RR1501-3.3*

Results

Some notable features of the results include the following:

- Even though we set the distance constraint at 60 minutes, only four of these schools are farther than half an hour away from the nearest ROTC host program, and only four are not affiliated with Army ROTC hosts. This may explain why most of these schools do not have their own ROTC programs: They are very close to and affiliated with existing ROTC hosts.
- Seventeen of the schools are in California or New York.
- Most of the schools are public universities but not state flagship schools, which tend to already have ROTC programs.

Map

For Scenario #1, we have also created the following map, Figure 3.4, as another way of showing the results. The program does not generate the map directly. However, it is possible to get the longitude and latitude of the selected schools from the Excel worksheet by unhiding the "Intermediate Output I" tab: "Point X" and "Point Y" are the columns that represent the location of a school. By using these data in conjunction with ArcGIS or another type of geographical software, it is possible to create maps like the one in Figure 3.4. A benefit of this type of mapping is that it makes it more apparent where suggested expansion sites are located: in this case, they are concentrated in New York and California.

Figure 3.4
Top 25 Schools for Possible Expansion or Supplemental Sites Ranked by Desirability Score and Restricted to Schools Within One Hour's Driving Time to the Nearest Host School

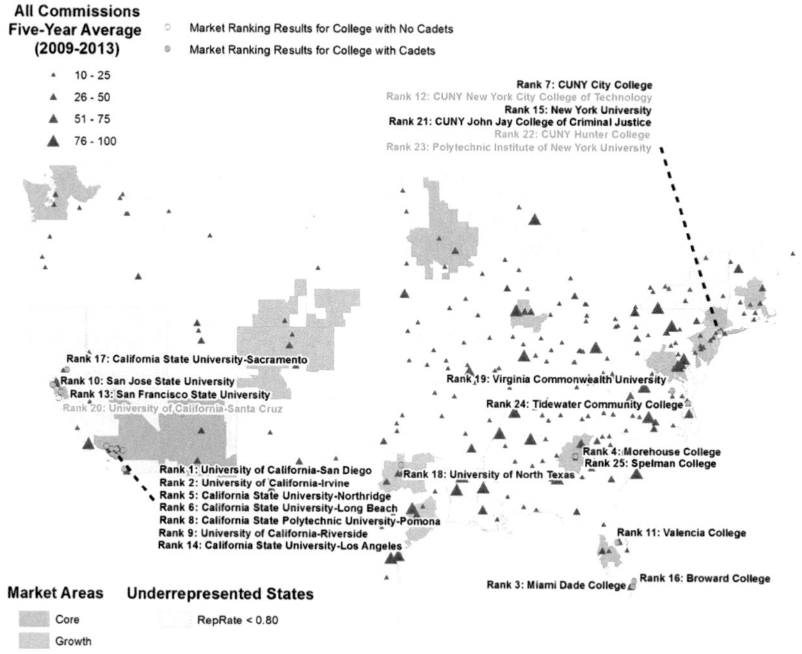

RAND *RR1501-3.4*

Scenario #2: Using All Strategic Objectives but Focusing on Diversity, Looking for Schools Within an Hour of Existing Programs

This scenario is like Scenario #1 in that we include all "Strategic Objectives," look only for schools within an hour of existing ROTC host programs, and include all states and ROTC affiliate statuses. However, in this scenario we also particularly prioritize "Demographic Diversity," assigning a "Weight" of "5" to each of the diversity "Indicator" variables and "1" to all others.

Setup

For setup, as just noted, we prioritize each of the diversity variables at "5" and all other "Strategic Objectives" "Indicator" variables at "1." We input a value of "0" for "Minimum Distance" and "60" for "Maximum Distance," to include in our results only those schools that are within an hour's driving time of existing ROTC host programs. We include "All States," select "Both" for all of the ROTC variables to include schools that are affiliated with ROTC programs and schools that are not, and input "500" and "100,000" for "Minimum Enrollment" and "Maximum Enrollment." Figure 3.5 shows what the program looks like with these settings selected.

Figure 3.5
Input Parameters for Scenario #2

Strategic Objectives	Indicator	Weight
Potential Production	Propensity	1
	Commissions	1
	Potential Productivity	1
	Market Potential	1
	Future Enrollment	1
Demographic Diversity	Magnitude	5
	Representation	5
	Diversity Index	5
Academic Quality	Selectivity	1
	Reputation	1
	STEM	1
Efficiency	Retention Score	1
	Community Support Score	1

Optional Constraints	Indicator	Value
Location	Minimum Distance (in minutes)	0
	Maximum Distance (in minutes)	60
	State	All States
ROTC Program	Army ROTC Affiliation	Both
	Air Force ROTC Status	Both
	Navy ROTC Status	Both
Size	Minimum Enrollment	500
	Maximum Enrollment	100,000

After you are finished entering your weights, press Ctrl-A to update the output.

RAND *RR1501-3.5*

Results

The results of this query are shown in Figure 3.6. Compared with the results from Figure 3.3, in which diversity was not prioritized more than other objectives, we see the following:

- Of the 25 results from Scenario #1, 21 also are listed in Scenario #2.
- This means that the majority of the results still are within half an hour of existing ROTC host programs, and almost all still are ROTC-affiliated schools.
- The results still are clustered in New York and California.
- The additional schools listed are California State University, San Bernardino; California State University, Dominguez Hills; California State University, East Bay; and Stony Brook University. These all are schools with very large minority student populations, and most have significant representation from at least five racial/ethnic groups.

Figure 3.6
Results from Scenario #2

Top 25 Schools for Possible Expansion Ranked by Desirability Score								
Rank	School	Nearest Host School	Distance (minutes)	State	ROTC Affiliate	Air Force ROTC	Navy ROTC	Enrollment
1	Miami Dade College	Florida International University	18	FL	Yes	Affiliate	No	25,750
2	California State University-Long Beach	California State University-Fullerton	27	CA	Yes	No	No	25,810
3	California State University-Northridge	University of California-Los Angeles	23	CA	Yes	No	No	25,536
4	University of California-Irvine	California State University-Fullerton	27	CA	Yes	No	No	21,876
5	University of California-San Diego	San Diego State University	23	CA	Yes	Affiliate	Affiliate	21,969
6	University of California-Riverside	Claremont McKenna College	31	CA	Yes	No	No	18,052
7	San Francisco State University	University of San Francisco	9	CA	Yes	No	No	22,218
8	San Jose State University	Santa Clara University	9	CA	Yes	Host	No	20,271
9	California State Polytechnic University-Pomona	Claremont McKenna College	15	CA	Yes	No	No	17,816
10	California State University-Los Angeles	University of Southern California	11	CA	Yes	No	No	14,979
11	California State University-Sacramento	University of California-Davis	24	CA	Yes	Host	No	20,603
12	CUNY City College	Fordham University	9	NY	Yes	No	No	9,421
13	CUNY New York City College of Technology	St. John's University-New York	14	NY	No	No	No	9,945
14	Valencia College	University of Central Florida	19	FL	Yes	No	No	15,749
15	New York University	St. John's University-New York	16	NY	Yes	Affiliate	No	20,950
16	Broward College	Florida International University	40	FL	Yes	Affiliate	No	12,100
17	California State University-San Bernardino	Claremont McKenna College	29	CA	Yes	Host	No	14,095
18	CUNY John Jay College of Criminal Justice	Fordham University	12	NY	Yes	No	No	10,269
19	University of North Texas	Texas Christian University	41	TX	Yes	Host	No	23,870
20	University of California-Santa Cruz	Santa Clara University	52	CA	No	No	No	15,562
21	CUNY Hunter College	Fordham University	13	NY	No	No	No	11,910
22	Virginia Commonwealth University	University of Richmond	12	VA	Yes	No	No	19,511
23	California State University-East Bay	University of California-Berkeley	27	CA	Yes	Affiliate	No	10,000
24	Stony Brook University	Hofstra University	50	NY	Yes	No	No	14,437
25	California State University-Dominguez Hills	University of Southern California	17	CA	Yes	No	No	7,799

RAND *RR1501-3.6*

Scenario #3: Using All Strategic Objectives, Looking for Schools Within an Hour of Existing Programs—but in Texas

In this scenario, as in Scenario #1, we are not prioritizing any of the individual "Strategic Objectives" over others, but just looking in general for high-potential schools within an hour of existing ROTC host programs. However, here, we are only looking for schools in Texas, a market of particular interest to USACC in which it wants to maintain or increase its presence.

Setup

Setup, as shown in Figure 3.7, looks the same as for Scenario #1, except that the "State" constraint is set to Texas ("TX").

Figure 3.7
Input Parameters for Scenario #3

Strategic Objectives	Indicator	Weight
Potential Production	Propensity	1
	Commissions	1
	Potential Productivity	1
	Market Potential	1
	Future Enrollment	1
Demographic Diversity	Magnitude	1
	Representation	1
	Diversity Index	1
Academic Quality	Selectivity	1
	Reputation	1
	STEM	1
Efficiency	Retention Score	1
	Community Support Score	1

Optional Constraints	Indicator	Value
Location	Minimum Distance (in minutes)	0
	Maximum Distance (in minutes)	60
	State	TX
ROTC Program	Army ROTC Affiliation	Both
	Air Force ROTC Status	Both
	Navy ROTC Status	Both
Size	Minimum Enrollment	500
	Maximum Enrollment	100,000

After you are finished entering your weights, press Ctrl-A to update the output.

RAND *RR1501-3.7*

Results

The results of this query are shown in Figure 3.8. Some notable features of the results include the following:

- Unlike the results for Scenario #1, which was based on the same query except on a national scale, nine of these results are for schools that are more than 30 minutes away from hosts, and one is close to an hour away. This suggests that the distance constraint might be somewhat more binding in a given state, as it is in Texas, than it is on a national scale. (And, indeed, if we were to increase the distance constraint to 120 minutes, five additional desirable schools would be included.)
- Twenty of the 25 result institutions are affiliates of ROTC programs.
- Because we are selecting from the 52 schools in Texas (only 26 of which are within an hour of an ROTC host program) rather than the 1,146 schools overall, the program had to go a lot lower in terms of desirability scores. Consequently, there is a lot more heterogeneity in the results: although the results include some big public universities, they also include smaller schools, private schools (including religious schools), and all-women schools.

Figure 3.8
Results from Scenario #3

Top 25 Schools for Possible Expansion Ranked by Desirability Score								
Rank	School	Nearest Host School	Distance (minutes)	State	ROTC Affiliate	Air Force ROTC	Navy ROTC	Enrollment
1	University of North Texas	Texas Christian University	41	TX	Yes	Host	No	23,870
2	The University of Texas at Dallas	The University of Texas at Arlington	43	TX	No	Affiliate	No	9,506
3	University of Houston-Downtown	University of Houston	9	TX	Yes	No	No	6,748
4	El Paso Community College	The University of Texas at El Paso	12	TX	Yes	No	No	10,325
5	Rice University	University of Houston	10	TX	Yes	Affiliate	Affiliate	3,775
6	San Antonio College	St. Mary's University	8	TX	Yes	No	No	5,422
7	Texas Woman's University	Texas Christian University	44	TX	No	No	No	6,275
8	Texas Southern University	University of Houston	5	TX	Yes	Affiliate	Affiliate	5,905
9	University of the Incarnate Word	St. Mary's University	12	TX	Yes	Affiliate	No	4,347
10	Southern Methodist University	The University of Texas at Arlington	31	TX	Yes	Affiliate	No	5,992
11	Del Mar College	Texas A & M University-Corpus Christi	14	TX	Yes	No	No	3,313
12	University of St Thomas	University of Houston	9	TX	Yes	No	No	1,242
13	Trinity University	St. Mary's University	12	TX	Yes	Affiliate	No	2,246
14	University of Dallas	The University of Texas at Arlington	24	TX	Yes	Affiliate	No	1,329
15	Saint Edward's University	The University of Texas at Austin	9	TX	Yes	Affiliate	No	3,449
16	University of Houston-Clear Lake	University of Houston	27	TX	Yes	No	No	2,105
17	Texas Lutheran University	Texas State University-San Marcos	38	TX	No	No	No	1,245
18	Wayland Baptist University	Texas Tech University	49	TX	Yes	No	No	1,210
19	Lubbock Christian University	Texas Tech University	7	TX	Yes	Affiliate	No	1,334
20	Huston-Tillotson University	The University of Texas at Austin	5	TX	Yes	No	Affiliate	802
21	Texas A & M University-Galveston	University of Houston	50	TX	No	No	Affiliate	1,761
22	Southwestern Adventist University	Texas Christian University	36	TX	No	No	No	618
23	University of Mary Hardin-Baylor	The University of Texas at Austin	58	TX	Yes	Affiliate	No	2,649
24	Our Lady of the Lake University-San Antonio	St. Mary's University	5	TX	Yes	No	No	1,209
25	Dallas Baptist University	The University of Texas at Arlington	20	TX	Yes	Affiliate	No	2,420

RAND *RR1501-3.8*

Scenario #4: Using All Strategic Objectives, Looking for Schools Within an Hour of Existing Programs, Excluding Schools with Air Force or Navy ROTC Programs

As true in Scenario #1, in Scenario #4, we do not prioritize any of the "Strategic Objectives" over others, but just look in general for high-potential schools within an hour of existing ROTC host programs. However, in this case we exclude schools that either host or affiliate with Navy or Air Force ROTC programs.

Setup

For setup, we prioritize each of the "Strategic Objectives" "Indicator" variables at "1," enter "0" for "Minimum Distance" and "60" for "Maximum Distance," include "All States," select "Both" for "Army ROTC Affiliation," "No" for both "Air Force ROTC Status" and "Navy ROTC Status," and input "500" and "100,000" for "Minimum Enrollment" and "Maximum Enrollment." Figure 3.9 shows the input parameters with these settings selected.

Figure 3.9
Input Parameters for Scenario #4

Strategic Objectives	Indicator	Weight
Potential Production	Propensity	1
	Commissions	1
	Potential Productivity	1
	Market Potential	1
	Future Enrollment	1
Demographic Diversity	Magnitude	1
	Representation	1
	Diversity Index	1
Academic Quality	Selectivity	1
	Reputation	1
	STEM	1
Efficiency	Retention Score	1
	Community Support Score	1

Optional Constraints	Indicator	Value
Location	Minimum Distance (in minutes)	0
	Maximum Distance (in minutes)	60
	State	All States
ROTC Program	Army ROTC Affiliation	Both
	Air Force ROTC Status	No
	Navy ROTC Status	No
Size	Minimum Enrollment	500
	Maximum Enrollment	100,000

After you are finished entering your weights, press Ctrl-A to update the output.

RAND *RR1501-3.9*

Results

The results of this query are shown in Figure 3.10. Some notable features of the results include the following:

- The exclusion of schools that participate in another service's ROTC program removes nine of the 25 results from Scenario #1, meaning that there still is significant overlap between these two sets of results. (The bottom nine schools here are those that did not appear in the results from Scenario #1.)
- As is also true for Scenario #1, the selected schools are concentrated in New York and California, including the nine schools that were not included in Scenario #1's results.
- As is also true for Scenario #1, most of the schools selected already are affiliated with Army ROTC programs. Most also are within 30 minutes of the nearest Army ROTC host, including most of the nine schools that were not in Scenario #1's results.

Figure 3.10
Results from Scenario #4

Top 25 Schools for Possible Expansion Ranked by Desirability Score

Rank	School	Nearest Host School	Distance (minutes)	State	ROTC Affiliate	Air Force ROTC	Navy ROTC	Enrollment
1	University of California-Irvine	California State University-Fullerton	27	CA	Yes	No	No	21,876
2	California State University-Northridge	University of California-Los Angeles	23	CA	Yes	No	No	25,536
3	California State University-Long Beach	California State University-Fullerton	27	CA	Yes	No	No	25,810
4	CUNY City College	Fordham University	9	NY	Yes	No	No	9,421
5	California State Polytechnic University-Pomona	Claremont McKenna College	15	CA	Yes	No	No	17,816
6	University of California-Riverside	Claremont McKenna College	31	CA	Yes	No	No	18,052
7	Valencia College	University of Central Florida	19	FL	Yes	No	No	15,749
8	CUNY New York City College of Technology	St. John's University-New York	14	NY	No	No	No	9,945
9	San Francisco State University	University of San Francisco	9	CA	Yes	No	No	22,218
10	California State University-Los Angeles	University of Southern California	11	CA	Yes	No	No	14,979
11	Virginia Commonwealth University	University of Richmond	12	VA	Yes	No	No	19,511
12	University of California-Santa Cruz	Santa Clara University	52	CA	No	No	No	15,562
13	CUNY John Jay College of Criminal Justice	Fordham University	12	NY	Yes	No	No	10,269
14	CUNY Hunter College	Fordham University	13	NY	No	No	No	11,910
15	Polytechnic Institute of New York University	St. John's University-New York	14	NY	No	No	No	1,927
16	Tidewater Community College	Norfolk State University	3	VA	Yes	No	No	11,563
17	CUNY College of Staten Island	Seton Hall University	22	NY	No	No	No	9,896
18	University at Buffalo	Canisius College	13	NY	Yes	No	No	17,573
19	Stony Brook University	Hofstra University	50	NY	Yes	No	No	14,437
20	CUNY Medgar Evers College	St. John's University-New York	19	NY	No	No	No	4,140
21	DeVry University-California	Claremont McKenna College	12	CA	Yes	No	No	4,165
22	Fullerton College	California State University-Fullerton	4	CA	Yes	No	No	4,046
23	Georgia Gwinnett College	Georgia State University	33	GA	Yes	No	No	6,543
24	Cooper Union for the Advancement of Science and Art	St. John's University-New York	16	NY	No	No	No	848
25	Long Island University-Brooklyn Campus	St. John's University-New York	14	NY	No	No	No	4,300

RAND *RR1501-3.10*

Scenario #5: Using All Strategic Objectives, Looking for Schools Not Within an Hour of Existing Programs

In this scenario, we do not prioritize any of the particular "Strategic Objectives" over others, but just look in general for high-potential schools that are not within an hour of existing ROTC host programs. These are schools that might be good candidates to host ROTC programs, but would not be good candidates for affiliating with ROTC programs because they are too far away from current hosts for students to reasonably commute.

Setup

For setup, we weight each of the "Strategic Objectives" "Indicator" variables at "1," enter "60" for "Minimum Distance" and "3,000" for "Maximum Distance," and include "All States." We select "No" for "Army ROTC Affiliation" and "Both" for the Navy and Air Force ROTC variables to exclude schools which are affiliated with Army ROTC but include schools that are affiliated with other ROTC programs. For consistency, we input "500" and "100,000" for "Minimum Enrollment" and "Maximum Enrollment." Figure 3.11 shows the input parameters with these settings selected. One could argue that for a new host program (rather than an affiliate) the size should be larger than 500, so that 15 commissions annually would be a more reasonable goal. We note, however, that only two of the schools selected in Scenario #5 have fewer than 1,000 students, and one barely so. We also note the possibility of forming affiliations with nearby schools to support commission production.

Figure 3.11
Input Parameters for Scenario #5

Strategic Objectives	Indicator	Weight
Potential Production	Propensity	1
	Commissions	1
	Potential Productivity	1
	Market Potential	1
	Future Enrollment	1
Demographic Diversity	Magnitude	1
	Representation	1
	Diversity Index	1
Academic Quality	Selectivity	1
	Reputation	1
	STEM	1
Efficiency	Retention Score	1
	Community Support Score	1

Optional Constraints	Indicator	Value
Location	Minimum Distance (in minutes)	60
	Maximum Distance (in minutes)	3,000
	State	All States
ROTC Program	Army ROTC Affiliation	No
	Air Force ROTC Status	Both
	Navy ROTC Status	Both
Size	Minimum Enrollment	500
	Maximum Enrollment	100,000

After you are finished entering your weights, press Ctrl-A to update the output.

RAND *RR1501-3.11*

Results

The results of this query are shown in Figure 3.12. Because we set the "Minimum Distance" at "60" minutes, the results that appear here do not appear in any other scenario.[5] In addition, we find the following:

- There is a great deal of geographical variation in these results. The schools are not just concentrated in New York and California but instead are spread throughout the country, particularly in the West, Southwest, and Midwest.
- Excluding schools within 60 minutes of an existing ROTC host program represents a substantial geographical limit for this set of priorities (objective weights) and constraints. Only eight of these schools would make a top-25 list of sites for expansion or supplementation of existing ROTC participants if we held all the weights and constraints constant except for dropping the 60-minute minimum-driving-distance requirement. In other words, it is possible that most of the best candidates for ROTC expansion or supplementation, given a specific set of user preferences, will be within an hour of existing host programs.

[5] Technically, a school exactly 60 minutes from a host could be on both lists. However, driving time is a continuous variable, so no school is exactly 60 minutes from a host.

Figure 3.12
Results from Scenario #5

Top 25 Schools for Possible Expansion Ranked by Desirability Score

Rank	School	Nearest Host School	Distance (minutes)	State	ROTC Affiliate	Air Force ROTC	Navy ROTC	Enrollment
1	Florida Gulf Coast University	Florida International University	135	FL	No	No	No	9,697
2	New Mexico Institute of Mining and Technology	University of New Mexico-Main Campus	74	NM	No	No	No	1,359
3	Montana Tech of the University of Montana	Montana State University	87	MT	No	No	No	1,683
4	California State University-Chico	University of California-Davis	125	CA	No	No	No	14,014
5	University of Wisconsin-Platteville	University of Wisconsin-Madison	90	WI	No	No	No	7,013
6	Valdosta State University	University of Florida	107	GA	No	Affiliate	No	8,837
7	Western Washington University	University of Washington-Seattle Campus	83	WA	No	No	No	12,835
8	Lamar University	University of Houston	90	TX	No	No	No	7,005
9	University of North Carolina Wilmington	Campbell University	117	NC	No	No	No	11,179
10	University of West Georgia	Georgia State University	61	GA	No	Affiliate	No	8,061
11	Wichita State University	Oklahoma State University-Main Campus	136	KS	No	No	No	8,430
12	California State University-Bakersfield	University of California-Los Angeles	111	CA	No	No	No	6,357
13	Humboldt State University	University of Oregon	313	CA	No	No	No	7,014
14	California State University-Stanislaus	University of California-Berkeley	101	CA	No	No	No	6,320
15	Caribbean University-Ponce	University of Puerto Rico-Mayaguez	60	PR	No	No	No	967
16	University of Minnesota-Duluth	University of Minnesota-Twin Cities	150	MN	No	Host	No	9,035
17	Angelo State University	Tarleton State University	219	TX	No	Host	No	5,033
18	The University of Texas at Tyler	Stephen F Austin State University	126	TX	No	No	No	4,071
19	Southeast Missouri State University	Southern Illinois University Carbondale	77	MO	No	Affiliate	No	8,014
20	Yale University	University of Connecticut	65	CT	No	Host	Affiliate	5,393
21	Oregon Institute of Technology	University of Oregon	263	OR	No	No	No	2,286
22	New Mexico Highlands University	University of New Mexico-Main Campus	116	NM	No	No	No	1,703
23	Fort Lewis College	University of New Mexico-Main Campus	294	CO	No	No	No	3,477
24	Western New Mexico University	New Mexico State University-Main Campus	131	NM	No	No	No	1,467
25	Southeastern Louisiana University	Louisiana State University and Agricultural & Mechanical College	62	LA	No	Affiliate	Affiliate	10,457

RAND *RR1501-3.12*

Conclusion

The ROTC-SET allows users flexibility in prioritizing different "Strategic Objectives" and "Indicator" variables in order to select colleges for new or expanded ROTC programs. There are 13 possible "Indicator" variables based on school-level, county-level, and state-level data, as well as comparisons with schools with existing ROTC programs. Users can weight each of these indicators as they prefer, as well as filter schools through "Optional Constraints" by how long it would take to drive from a school to the nearest ROTC host program, what state it is in, its current involvement with ROTC programs, and the size of its student body.

CHAPTER FOUR

Conclusions and Recommendations

The ROTC program currently accounts for about two-thirds of Regular Army officer production. Given current fiscal constraints, the Army can no longer afford to maintain ROTC units that do not commission the requisite number of fully-qualified officers. As the student population has shifted and resources have tightened, there is a need to reexamine both the productivity and location of units to ensure that Army ROTC attracts and commissions highly-qualified officers. At the same time, the Army needs to examine where resources garnered from downsized or closed units should be reinvested into the expansion or opening of other units. These assessments will be important in near-term operational and longer-term strategic deliberations and decisions concerning the "reposturing" of the ROTC program.

In this report, we have discussed results likely to emerge through the ROTC Program Review Process, and how they might be improved using two strategic planning tools: the Reserve Officers' Training Corps Program Evaluation Tool (ROTC-PET) and the ROTC Selection Evaluation Tool (ROTC-SET).

Planning Tools

Both the ROTC-PET and the ROTC-SET allow policy planners to explore the potential effects of different sets of "Strategic Objectives" and various environmental scenarios using information on existing ROTC programs, colleges, and the areas surrounding colleges. The ROTC-PET allows users to evaluate existing ROTC programs, including both the school that is hosting the program and the other schools that participate as feeders or affiliates. The ROTC-SET allows users to evaluate schools that do not currently host ROTC programs, to help guide the selection of schools to either host new ROTC programs or participate in existing ROTC programs.

To evaluate existing ROTC programs, planners can use the ROTC-PET to simulate scenarios that include up to six "Strategic Objectives": optimizing "Production," "Academic Quality," "Demographic Diversity," "Efficiency," "Cost," and the "Quality of Commissions." In each simulation, users are required to explicitly set their assumptions about the operational environment. This includes the "Strategic Objectives" they wish the algorithm to include; the relative priorities of the 11 associated indicators; the unit of evaluation (host or individual school); a mission allocation rule across brigades (variable or fixed at historical levels); a desired total commission number; their assumption about the extent of "Untapped Productivity"; and whether they want to include one or more of the Army evaluation criteria in the simulation.

In order to select new schools for participation in ROTC or to expand existing sites with cadets, the ROTC-SET also gives planners a variety of possible objectives and constraints. The possible objectives to be optimized are related to "Potential Production," "Demographic Diversity," "Academic Quality," and "Efficiency." Users also can choose whether to exclude schools that are not within a set driving time of an existing ROTC program, schools that are not in a particular state, those that do (or do not) currently affiliate with Army ROTC programs or host or affiliate with ROTC programs from other services, or those with enrollments outside the minimum or maximum numbers defined by the user.

Results and Recommendations

Based on the results of our simulations, such as those illustrated below, in Table 4.1, we recommend that the Army use the planning tools to evaluate existing ROTC programs and explore new market opportunities; to keep up with changes in the college student population; to integrate the ROTC Program Review Process, to enhance the Army's capability to accomplish GAO's recommended actions; and to help meet the Army's near-term and longer-term strategic goals for its ROTC program, the largest commissioning source for officers, including the optimal use of its resources.

The ROTC-PET enhances the Army's capability to evaluate the performance of its ROTC host programs and schools with cadets connected with these hosts, by allowing planners to discern the potential negative impact of underperforming programs. Based on the planner's strategic objectives, the relative priority of these objectives, and explicitly-stated assumptions about the operational environment, the ROTC-PET also provides ways to mitigate negative effects. Table 4.1 summarizes a few key results for the scenarios discussed in this report. The results in Table 4.1 show how the ROTC-PET enhances the Army's capability for near-term operational and longer-term strategic planning and decisionmaking. In Scenario #1, when we apply the 2014 Army evaluation criteria and approach, results from the Risk Analysis of the ROTC-PET show that scholarship cost will increase by 2.2 percent and representation of racial/ethnic minorities among commissions will decrease by 2.6 percent, both undesirable outcomes. In Scenario #2, we simulate a solution that produces the required number of commissions and complies with the 2014 Army evaluation criteria, while minimizing scholarship cost per school and maximizing representation of minorities among commissions. The ROTC-PET produces a solution that eliminates the increase in scholarship cost and reverses the adverse effect on representation of minorities among commissions.

In Scenario #3, we use the ROTC-PET to find a solution that is driven solely by three objectives (commission production, minority representation among commissions, and scholarship cost per host); it is allowed to vary mission allocation across brigades from the recent historical allocation and, to a degree (0.5 standard deviation), to increase production at individual host schools. Given the inputs made in Scenario #3, the Army ROTC program *improves* representation of racial/ethnic minorities by 8.4 percent, while only increasing

Table 4.1
Key Results from Scenarios Illustrating Usage of the Reserve Officers' Training Corps Program Evaluation Tool (Changes as Percentages)

Scenario	Description	Scholarship Cost per Host	Racial/Ethnic Minority Representation Among Commissions	Percentage STEM Among Commissions
1	Apply the 2014 Army ROTC evaluation criteria and methodology + fixed historical mission allocation across brigades + 0 untapped productivity	+2.2	–2.6	+1.2
2	Army criteria + optimize scholarship cost + minority representation + fixed historical mission allocation across brigades + 0 untapped productivity	–0.3	+1.4	–0.9
3	Optimize production + minority representation + scholarship cost + vary mission allocation across brigades + 0.5 untapped productivity	+0.6	+8.4	–3.5
4	Optimize production + STEM + minority representation + scholarship cost + vary mission allocation across brigades + 0.5 untapped productivity	+4.0	+8.8	+4.1

scholarship cost per host by 0.6 percent. STEM commissions decline by 3.5 percent, however. In Scenario #4, we use the ROTC-PET to find a solution that is driven by four objectives (production, representation of STEM among commissions, minority representation among commissions, and scholarship cost per host) and is allowed to vary mission allocation across brigades and production at individual hosts as described for Scenario #3. In Scenario #4, the Army ROTC program improves racial/ethnic minority representation by 8.8 percent and STEM by 4.1 percent, though in doing so it increases scholarship cost by 4 percent. We note that the application of the ROTC-PET in the more strategic manner suggested in Scenarios #3 and #4 demonstrates the tool's ability to accept new criteria, rather than the more restrictive criteria applied in Scenarios #1 and #2.

The ROTC-SET is designed to help the Army find colleges and universities that are not currently hosting ROTC programs but which can provide cadets with desired characteristics based on a given set of objectives This includes both current non-host programs with cadets (expansion) as well as new schools with no current ROTC cadets (supplementation). Using the four "Strategic Objectives" ("Potential Production," "Demographic Diversity," "Academic Quality," and "Efficiency") and assigning the relative importance (from 0 to 10) of their 13 "Indicator" variables, planners can generate a list of high-potential colleges and universities. The ROTC-SET also can be used to identify top schools to meet such objectives within a given state, among schools with or without current cadets (Army, Navy, or Air Force), within a set driving time of existing host programs, and of a particular size.

APPENDIX A

Methodology of the Reserve Officers' Training Corps Program Evaluation Tool

Installation

The ROTC-PET can be accessed via a DVD. Potential users needing a copy of the ROTC-PET can request one from USACC. The text below is also in the "Readme" file, which is on the DVD. To run the application properly, all files and sub-folders must remain within the ROTC-PET folder and the ROTC-PET folder must be placed in the Desktop directory. The only requirements for use of this tool are a Windows PC[1] and a recently updated web browser, though Internet access is not necessary. Once users have met these requirements they can access the ROTC-PET by double-clicking the file, "run PET.bat." A prompt screen will open followed by the default browser with the tool loaded to the "Inputs" tab of the ROTC-PET. While using the tool, do not close the prompt screen; when finished using the ROTC-PET users should simply close the browser and the prompt screen will go away.

The remainder of this appendix describes some of the mathematics behind the ROTC-PET. It is not necessary to understand the math in order to either use the ROTC-PET or modify the data or code.

---

[1] PET can be accessed on a MAC, however the user would need to download his/her own copy of R, install required packages, and open the tool using commands within R. For more about R, see R Foundation, undated, and RStudio, undated.

The Continuous Knapsack Problem

Readers familiar with operations research will likely find it easiest to understand the ROTC-PET tool after seeing the mathematical program underlying our methodology. Let us index academic institutions with the letter j and use x_j decision variables representing the officer production rate assigned to institution j. We have calculated the normalized metrics listed above using historical data, essentially grading ROTC programs in various ways. Let $a_{i,j}$ terms refer to the mark given to institution j when considering metric i. We reserve the use of Greek letters for ROTC-PET model parameters for which we anticipate user input. Here, α_i terms represent the weight given to metric i within the ROTC-PET framework. The user is free to repeatedly adjust these terms and inspect the resulting assignments of cadets to institutions, as well as the effect on overall national outcomes, such as the proportion of minorities among commissioned cadets.

The user also specifies the goal for total ROTC officer production. We label this model parameter β. Note that each academic institution has a historical officer production rate. We use b_j to refer to the mean production rate at institution j and c_j to refer to the standard deviation of production at institution j, both as measured over the past five years. The user can specify a model parameter γ that defines the number of standard deviations above the mean that separates plausible from implausible production levels at each institution.

Given the notation defined above, we provide the following mathematical program. The objective function maximizes the sum of the institution-specific metrics weighted by user-defined, metric-specific weights and institution-specific production targets. Constraint (1) then ensures that overall production is set to reach the user-identified target level. Constraint (2) ensures that each institution is assigned a plausible production target, both nonnegative and less than would be implausible given historical production rates:

$$\max_{x} \sum_{i} \sum_{j} \alpha_i \alpha_{i,j} x_j,$$

such that

1. $\sum_j x_j = \beta$.
2. $0 \le x_j \le b_j + \gamma c_j \quad \forall j$.

The mathematical program shown above is a specific instance of what operations researchers have dubbed the continuous knapsack problem. In this class of problem, we are filling a knapsack with materials of different values in order to maximize the total value of the contents. For this particular problem, the different "materials" are cadets from different institutions, and the values are how well they perform on the strategic objectives. What makes this "continuous" is that we can fill the knapsack with fractional amounts of each material or, in this case, that we can use some cadets from a particular institution without having to use the maximum possible number of cadets from that institution. The general form for solving this problem is to select the most valuable material first and use all of it, and then go to the next-most valuable material, until the knapsack is full. That is essentially what we are doing here: filling up our production of officer commissions with the school that performs the best on the "Strategic Objectives"—or has the highest desirability score—and then going to the next-best-performing school on down, until our production of officer commissions is full.

We solve the problem as follows. First, we sort institutions by the benefit we get from assigning officers to the institution, measured in terms of $\sum_i \alpha_i \alpha_{i,j}$ for institution j. The top institution is the institution that performs the best on the weighted average of the strategic objectives; the bottom institution is the institution that performs the worst. The program starts with β officers to assign. It goes sequentially through the list of institutions in rank order, starting with the institution offering the most benefit per officer. It assigns each school to produce the school's maximum production, unless the school's maximum production is higher than the remaining number of officers to assign, in which case the school is assigned to produce the remaining number of officers. The program then goes to the second-highest institution and repeats the process until all of the officers have been assigned.

The mathematical program shown above reflects the most basic version of the cadet assignment problem that is solved via the ROTC-PET. We allow the user to specify additional constraints—for example, ensuring that each ROTC brigade is assigned to produce the same proportion of commissions that it has historically produced. With that constraint, the program would perform rankings and assignments for schools within each brigade, as opposed to doing one overall optimization function. Crucially, none of the additional complications we consider are much more difficult to solve than the continuous knapsack problem. For example, fixing brigade production breaks the problem identified above into brigade-specific problems that are each separate instances of the continuous knapsack problem.

Solving the identified optimization problem and its variants sometimes results in unrealistically-small officer production targets for one or more academic institutions. This issue is particularly relevant when the user seeks to find a distribution for a relatively-small number of officers, nationwide. To mitigate this problem, we created an alternative methodology for just this case. The model parameter β is set to the historical nationwide officer production rate. The continuous knapsack problem is solved. Next, academic institutions are ranked in the order of their current production targets, from smallest to largest. The production targets for the ROTC programs being asked to produce the smallest numbers of officers are set to 0, iteratively, until we reach a point at which zeroing out the next-smallest program would leave us with less nationwide officer production than the user-defined target. In this analysis, any school that has a production target of 0 is considered underperforming, meaning that the tool recommends that it be closed.

As an example, consider setting the γ parameter to 0. This caps the target officer production rate at each institution at the institution's historical production rate. When we set the parameter β to a value, such as 5,160, that is close to the historical nationwide officer production rate, we have very little flexibility to move the officer production targets of each institution. Almost every institution must produce the number of officers it has historically produced and no more to allow us to both match the nationwide production target and ensure that no program produces more than it has historically. The only programs that are underperforming in such a scenario are schools that currently have an Army category of E (or possibly D), programs that are producing very few officers at the moment. This is true regardless of how the user weights the distinct criteria used to evaluate programs. As we lower the parameter β or increase the parameter γ, more programs are shut down. These schools might have a higher category using the Army's categorization schema; programs that are high-performing on the "Strategic Objectives" expand to pick up the increased capacity from shutting down the underperforming programs.

Host-Level and Army-Categorization Criteria–Based Analyses

As described above, the ROTC-PET user can perform host-level analysis optimizing the production targets assigned to different ROTC hosts. To enable this analysis, we define "Strategic Objectives" metrics for each host of "Efficiency," "Demographic Diversity," "Academic Quality," "Production," "Cost," and "Quality of Commissions." We do that by aggregating academic institution-specific data, weighting by institution production where appropriate, and then normalizing the results. For example, production at the institution level is measured in terms of the officers produced by each school. At the host level, we first add up all the officers produced at each institution assigned to the host and then normalize the results across the set of hosts. In contrast, academic quality at the host level is defined by taking the weighted average of the academic scores of the institutions assigned to a host, weighted by the number of officers that has been produced at each institution in the preceding five years. The result is then normalized across hosts.

The user of the ROTC-PET also can run analyses based on ROTC program categorization criteria that the Army has established. We use historical data to determine which programs achieve the requirements outlined by the Army. The user may require that our model assign commissions to these programs before considering assigning commissions to other programs. In addition, the tool calculates the categories that would be assigned to different programs using the Army's categorization criteria and assuming that individual academic institutions produce the number of officers assigned to them after solving an optimization problem of the type shown above.

APPENDIX B

Data Used to Construct the Measures in the Reserve Officers' Training Corps Program Evaluation Tool

This appendix describes the data used to develop the ROTC-PET.

Data Source

To construct the indicators in the ROTC-PET, we drew on multiple data sources. We describe each of the data sources in this section.

Integrated Postsecondary Education Data System (IPEDS)

The National Center for Education Statistics established the Integrated Postsecondary Education Data System in 1992 as its core postsecondary education data collection program. IPEDS defines postsecondary education programs as formal, open to the general public, and designed primarily for students beyond high school age. It does not collect information from any schools or entities whose primary purpose is not the provision of postsecondary education (e.g., non-credit continuing education programs and high schools with vocational programs only). It also excludes training sites at prisons, military bases, and corporations, which are not considered to be separate institutions or branches.

We used IPEDS data from the 2012 wave, when there were 7,735 schools in the database. We applied several exclusion rules, which resulted in including 1,419 schools in our evaluation tool.

We used the following variables from IPEDS:

- school quality: admissions selectivity, 75th percentile of SAT/ACT score

- student body: academic major
- institution profile: institution name and address, tuition and fees.

ROTC Administrative Data

ROTC administrative data provided by USACC include all cadets enrolled in ROTC programs nationwide from fall 2008 to spring 2013. Variables include demographic information (such as gender, race/ethnicity, and citizenship), scholarship status, longitudinal data on MS level and retention, and the school where cadets were enrolled. Information on the colleges attended by cadets allows the ROTC data to be matched with national data on higher education institutions. A total of 168,165 individuals are represented in ROTC administrative data.

U.S. News and World Report College Data

U.S. News and World Report provides data on college rankings and institution characteristics for more than 1,800 educational institutions. We used data from academic year 2012. The variables include acceptance rate and the 25th and 75th percentiles of SAT/ACT scores. The two variables were used as complements to the IPEDS data. When the IPEDS value was missing, we applied the *U.S. News and World Report* value.

Variables

From the data sources described in the previous section, we constructed multiple school-level, county-level, and state-level variables. We used the variables as inputs to calculate the 13 indicators. In Table B.1, we list each variable used, record the raw variable names and data sources, and describe the process of constructing the variables. The selection rules and variables that we used in the exclusion process are shown in Table B.1.

Table B.1
Reserve Officers' Training Corps Program Evaluation Tool Variables

Variable Description	Variable(s)	Dataset and Year(s)	Process Description
School name	instnm	IPEDS, 2012	None
Acceptance rate	admssn, applcn	IPEDS, *U.S. News and World Report*, 2012	Acceptance rate = admssn/applcn; if IPEDS acceptance rate from IPEDS is missing, use *U.S. News and World Report* data to fill in.
SAT 75th percentile	satvr75, satmt75, satwr75, actcm75	IPEDS, *U.S. News and World Report*, 2012	sat75 = satvr75 + satmt75 + satwr75; if SAT score is missing, use actcm75, and convert it to equivalent SAT score; if still missing, use *U.S. News and World Report* data to fill in.
Percentage of students in physical science and engineering majors	lstudy, cipcode, eftotlt	IPEDS, fall 2012	Keep if lstudy equals 23 and cipcode equals 140,000; the eftotlt is total enrollment of engineering majors. Keep if lstudy equals 23 and cipcode equals 400,000; the eftotlt is total enrollment of physical science majors. Sum the two enrollments to get total enrollment for these two types of majors, and then divide by total enrollment and multiply by 100 to get the percentage; the enrollment is also for full-time degree-/certificate-seeking undergraduates.
Total yearly expense (tuition + room and board)	tuition2, chg5ay3, chg7ay3	IPEDS, fall 2012	Expense = tuition2 + (chg5ay3 + chg7ay3)/2
Total cadet enrollment	cadet_id, acad_sch_cd	ROTC, fall 2012	Collapse the student-level ROTC enrollment data to the school level to get the cadet count.
Whether the school is ROTC host	rotc_sch_cd	ROTC, fall 2012	Identify all schools that appear in the ROTC commission dataset as ROTC hosts.
Average number of cadets 2009–2013	acad_sch_cd, rotc_sch_cd, sssn, comm_dt	ROTC, fall 2009–spring 2013	Count the number of cadets enrolled each year for each school, and compute the average.

Table B.1—Continued

Variable Description	Variable(s)	Dataset and Year(s)	Process Description
Tier	tier1	ROTC, fall 2009–spring 2013	None; this is USACC's past measure of top schools.
Average number of commissions	Acad_sch_cd, rotc_sch_cd, sssn, comm_dt, sclr_award_cd, ms_class	ROTC, fall 2009–spring 2013	Count the commissions each year for each school, and compute the average.
Average number of cadets with scholarships	acad_sch_cd, rotc_sch_cd, sssn, comm_dt, sclr_award_cd, ms_class	ROTC, fall 2009–spring 2013	Count the number of cadets with scholarships each year for each school, and compute the average.
Number of African American commissions 2009–2013	AfAm_FY09–AfAm_FY13	ROTC, fall 2009–spring 2013	Count the commissions each year for each school, and compute the average.
Number of other race commissions 2009–2013	AmInd_FY09–AmInd_FY13, AsianAm_FY09–AsianAm_FY13, Other_FY09–Other_FY13	ROTC, fall 2009–spring 2013	Count the commissions each year for each school, and compute the average.
Number of white commissions 2009–2013	Cauc_FY09–Cauc_FY13	ROTC, fall 2009–spring 2013	Count the commissions each year for each school, and compute the average.
Number of Hispanic commissions 2009–2013	Hispanic_FY09–Hispanic_FY13	ROTC, fall 2009–spring 2013	Count the commissions each year for each school, and compute the average.
Number of STEM-major cadets 2009–2013	stem_09–stem_13	ROTC, fall 2009–spring 2013	Count the commissions each year for each school, and compute the average.
Total personnel cost between 2009 and 2013	Total_FY0913_BN_Personnel	ROTC, fall 2009–spring 2013	None

Table B.1—Continued

Variable Description	Variable(s)	Dataset and Year(s)	Process Description
Is in a core market	Core..2014	ROTC, fall 2009–spring 2013	None
Is in a growth market	Growth..2014	ROTC, fall 2009–spring 2013	None
Meets USACC criteria	Representation. Rate..RepRate	ROTC, fall 2009–spring 2013	None
Order of Merit score	OMS_Score	ROTC, fall 2009–spring 2013	None
Brigade number	j	ROTC, fall 2009–spring 2013	None
Army-assigned categories to the host schools	category	ROTC, fall 2009–spring 2013	None
Public school	sector	IPEDS, 2012	None
School is residential school	ccsizset	IPEDS, 2012	None
In-state tuition	tuition2	IPEDS, 2012	None
Out-of-state tuition	tuition3	IPEDS, 2012	None
Room and board 2012–2013	chg5ay3, chg7ay3	IPEDS, 2012	None

APPENDIX C

Data Used to Construct the Measures in the Reserve Officers' Training Corps Selection Evaluation Tool

This appendix describes the data sources and variables we used to construct the indicators in the ROTC-SET.

Data Sources

To construct the indicators in the ROTC-SET, we drew on multiple data sources; we describe each data source in this section.

Integrated Postsecondary Education Data System

As discussed in Appendix B, the National Center for Education Statistics established the Integrated Postsecondary Education Data System in 1992 as its core postsecondary education data collection program. As is true for the ROTC-PET, for the ROTC-SET we used IPEDS data from the 2012 wave, when there were 7,735 schools in the database. We again applied several exclusion rules, which resulted in including 1,419 schools in our evaluation tool.

We used the following variables from IPEDS:

- school quality: admissions selectivity, housing and facilities, faculty, 75th percentile of SAT/ACT score
- geographic: campus settings
- student body: enrollment, academic major, gender, race/ethnicity distribution
- institution profile: institution name and address, educational services offerings, tuition and fees

- degrees awarded: field of study, level or type of degree, and length of the program, as well as demographic information on degree recipients.

The selection rules and variables that we used in the exclusion process are listed in Table C.1.

ROTC Administrative Data

As is true for the ROTC-PET, we used USACC-provided ROTC administrative data for cadets who were commissioned as officers in either 2011 or 2012.

U.S. Army Cadet Command On-Campus Survey Data

USACC provided data from its on-campus surveys that were conducted in 2002, 2004–2005, and 2006, generating a sample of 15,322 students at 121 college campuses. The survey was designed to evaluate individual

Table C.1
Reserve Officers' Training Corps Selection Evaluation Tool School Selection Rules and IPEDS Variables Used

Selection Rule	Variable	Dataset and Year	Description of Process
Drop schools that are not bachelor primary schools.	ccbasic	IPEDS, 2012	Drop if ccbasic equals 3, 9, 12, 13, 24, 25, 26, 27, 28, 29, 30, or 31.
Drop schools that are not Title IV.	pset4flg	IPEDS, 2012	Drop if pset4flg equals 2.
Keep schools that are for four or more years.	control	IPEDS, 2012	Keep if control equals 1–2.
Drop schools that are private for profit.	iclevel	IPEDS, 2012	Keep if iclevel equals 1.
Keep schools that are degree-granting.	instcat	IPEDS, 2012	Keep if instcat equals 2–3.
Drop non-traditional four-year schools.	carnegie	IPEDS, 2012	Drop if carnegie equals 40, 51, 52, 53, 56, 58, 59, or 60.
Drop schools without tenure systems.	tenursys	IPEDS, 2012	Drop if tenursys equals 2.

students' knowledge of, attitudes toward, and intentions to join ROTC programs. It also collected demographic information and students' enrollment status.

American Community Survey Public Use Microdata Sample

The American Community Survey (ACS) is an ongoing survey that is conducted every year. It samples a small percentage of the population and collects information on demographic characteristics, family structure, work, income, education, veteran status, and living conditions. The ACS Public Use Microdata Sample (PUMS) files provide a set of microvariables from the ACS at the individual or household level.

We used the 2012 ACS to create contextual variables. The variables include state unemployment rate, median household income, percentage of adults in the state with a college degree, percentage of military members in the state, and veterans per 1,000 state population.

U.S. News and World Report College Data

We used the same *U.S. News and World Report* data as for the ROTC-PET. In addition, we used the Peer Assessment score. This score, ranging from 1 to 5, is a rating of the academic quality of a school's undergraduate program by top college administrators.

Integrated Postsecondary Education Data System Analytics: Delta Cost Project Database

The IPEDS Analytics: Delta Cost Project Database is a longitudinal database reproduced from annual IPEDS surveys. The aim of the database is to harmonize and standardize the variables to address inter-wave changes in definitions and reporting formats, in order to ensure the integrity of long-term trends analysis. The database includes data on over 6,000 postsecondary institutions from academic years 1986–1987 to 2008–2009. The variables collected in the database include postsecondary financing, enrollment, staffing, completion, and student aid.

We used enrollment data from the Delta Cost Project Database. The specific variable is the total number of full-time first-time degree/certificate-seeking undergraduates. We also incorporated enrollment data from later waves of IPEDS to form a panel covering 25 years, which allows us to predict enrollment in the year 2020.

Variables

From the data sources described in the previous section, we constructed multiple school-level, county-level, and state-level variables. We used the variables as inputs to calculate the 13 indicators. In Tables C.2 and

Table C.2
ROTC-SET School-Level Variables

Variable Description	Variable(s)	Dataset and Year	Description of Process
School name	instnm	IPEDS, 2012	None
Whether the school is public	sector	IPEDS, 2012	School is public if sector equals 1.
Whether the school is residential	ccsizset	IPEDS, 2012	School is primarily residential or highly residential if ccsizset is 7, 8, 10, 11, 13, 14, 16, or 17; school is primarily non-residential if ccsizset is 6, 9, 12, or 15.
County of the school	countycd	IPEDS, 2012	None
Peer Assessment score	Peer Assessment score	*U.S. News and World Report*	The school's average score on a survey asking top college administrators to rate its undergraduate academic quality on a scale of 1 (marginal) to 5 (distinguished). The variable is from the *U.S. News and World Report* website.
Percentage of postsecondary teachers who are full time	staffcat, hrtotlt	IPEDS, 2012	Total postsecondary teachers is hrtotlt when staffcat equals 1,200; full-time postsecondary teachers is hrtotlt when staffcat equals 2,200; divide full-time total by grand total and multiply by 100 to get the percentage.

Table C.2—Continued

Variable Description	Variable(s)	Dataset and Year	Description of Process
Acceptance rate	admssn, applcn	IPEDS, *U.S. News and World Report*, 2012	Acceptance rate = admssn/applcn; if IPEDS acceptance rate from IPEDS is missing, use *U.S. News and World Report* data to fill in.
SAT 75th percentile	satvr75, satmt75, satwr75, actcm75	IPEDS, *U.S. News and World Report*, 2012	sat75 = satvr75 + satmt75 + satwr75; if SAT score is missing, use actcm75 and convert it to the equivalent SAT score. If still missing, use *U.S. News and World Report* data to fill in.
Total enrollment	efalevel, eftotlt	IPEDS, 2012	Keep if efalevel equals 23; the eftotlt is full-time degree/certificate-seeking undergraduates total.
Percentage of students in physical science and engineering majors	lstudy, cipcode, eftotlt	IPEDS, 2012	Keep if lstudy equals 23 and cipcode equals 140,000; the eftotlt is total enrollment of engineering majors. Keep if lstudy equals 23 and cipcode equals 400,000; the eftotlt is total enrollment of physical science majors. Sum the two enrollments to get total enrollment for these two types of majors, then divide by total enrollment and multiply by 100 to get the percentage; the enrollment is also for full-time degree- and certificate-seeking undergraduates.
Percentage of African American students	efalevel, efbkaat	IPEDS, 2012	Keep if efalevel equals 23; the efbkaat is full-time degree/certificate-seeking undergraduate total of African American students. Divide by total enrollment and multiply by 100 to get the percentage.

Table C.2—Continued

Variable Description	Variable(s)	Dataset and Year	Description of Process
Percentage of Hispanic students	efalevel, efhisp	IPEDS, 2012	Keep if efalevel equals 23; the efhisp is full-time degree/certificate-seeking undergraduate total of Hispanic students. Divide by total enrollment and multiply by 100 to get the percentage.
Percentage of male students	efalevel, eftotlm	IPEDS, 2012	Keep if efalevel equals 23; the eftotlm is full-time degree/certificate-seeking undergraduate total of male students. Divide by total enrollment and multiply by 100 to get the percentage.
Total yearly expense (tuition + room and board)	tuition2, chg5ay3, chg7ay3	IPEDS, 2012	Expense = tuition2 + (chg5ay3 + chg7ay3)/2
Total cadet enrollment	cadet_id, acad_sch_cd	ROTC, fall 2012	Collapse the student-level ROTC enrollment data to the school level to get the cadet count.
Total number of white cadets	cadet_id, acad_sch_cd, race_cd	ROTC, fall 2012	Keep the white non-Hispanic (race_cd = C and ethnic_cd ≠ 1, 4, 6, 9, or S) students; collapse the student-level enrollment data to school level to get the count.
Whether the school is an ROTC host	rotc_sch_cd	ROTC, fall 2012	Identify all schools that appear in the ROTC commission dataset as ROTC hosts.
Number of commissions	cadet_id	ROTC, spring 2013	Collapse the student-level ROTC commission data to the school level to get the commission count.
Driving time to nearest host			Driving time between each of two schools is generated by a geographic information system; identify the nearest host to get the time from a school to the nearest host.

Table C.2—Continued

Variable Description	Variable(s)	Dataset and Year	Description of Process
Graduation total	grtotl	IPEDS, 2012	Total number of students who graduated from a given school
Midwest Region	midwest	IPEDS, 2012	Dummy indicating whether a program is in the Midwest region (IA, IL, IN, KS, MI, MN, MO, ND, NE, OH, SD, WI)
Northeast Region	northeast	IPEDS, 2012	Dummy indicating whether a program is in the Northeast region (CT, MA, ME, NH, NJ, NY, PA, RI, VT)
South Region	south	IPEDS, 2012	Dummy indicating whether a program is in the South region (AL, AR, DC, DE, FL, GA, KY, LA, MD, MS, NC, OK, SC, TN, TX, VA, WV)
West Region	west	IPEDS, 2012	Dummy indicating whether a program in in the West region (AK, AZ, CA, CO, HI, ID, MT, NM, NV, OR, UT, WA, WY)
Percentage of instructors with doctorate or terminal degrees	phd	Petersons, 2010	Number of instructors with a doctorate degree over the total number of instructors. deg_term_n/tot_n*100

C.3, we list each variable used, record the raw variable names and data sources, and describe the process of constructing the variable.

We present school-level variables in Table C.2. These variables cover information in several categories: (1) institutional characteristics, including school name, whether the school is public, whether the school is residential,[1] and the location of the school; (2) school

---

[1] We applied the IPEDS' definition for school setting, which is based on the Carnegie Classification 2005 (Indiana University Center for Postsecondary Research, undated). The Carnegie Classification defines school setting based on the percentage of full-time undergraduate students living in institutionally-managed housing. In our analysis, schools that have less than 25 percent of enrollments consisting of degree-seeking undergraduates or less than 50 percent of students enrolled full time and living on campus are recorded as primarily nonresidential and otherwise residential.

Table C.3
ROTC-SET State-Level Variables

Variable Description	Variable(s)	Dataset and Year(s)	Description of Process
Unemployment rate	empstat, statefip	ACS, 2012	Keep if empstat equals 1 or 2, and collapse the microdata to get state-level labor-force population. Keep if empstat equals 2, and collapse the microdata to get state-level unemployed population. Divide the unemployed population by labor-force population and multiply by 100 to get the unemployment rate.
Median household income	hhincome, statefip	ACS, 2012	Collapse the microdata to get the state-level median household income.
Percentage of adults in the state with college degrees	age, educ, statefip	ACS, 2012	Keep if age ≥ 25, and collapse the microdata to get state-level adult population. Keep if educ ≥ 07, and collapse the microdata to get the state-level number of adults holding college degrees. Divide the total number of adults with college degrees by the adult population and multiply by 100 to get the percentage.
Postsecondary education appropriations per full-time equivalent	state appropriation, local appropriation, full-time equivalent	IPEDS, 2011	Sum the state and local appropriations, and divide by the total full-time equivalent.

Table C.3—Continued

Variable Description	Variable(s)	Dataset and Year(s)	Description of Process
Percentage of military members in the state	occ, statefip	ACS, 2012	Collapse the microdata to get the state population. Keep if occ equals 9,800, 9,810, 9,820, or 9,830, and collapse the microdata to get the state-level number of military members. Divide the number of military members by the state population and multiply by 100 to get the percentage.
Number of veterans within one hour's driving distance to the school		ACS, 2008–2012	Get the number of veterans by ZIP Code from the ACS, and use a geographic information system to compute the number of veterans within one hour's driving distance.
Accession rate	Accession_rate	DoD	New enlistments per 1,000 18–24 year olds into the services' active components

quality and selectivity, including Peer Assessment score, percentage of postsecondary teachers who are full time, acceptance rate, and the 75th percentile of SAT score; (3) student body, including total enrollment, percentage of minority students, and percentage of students in physical science and engineering majors; (4) information on tuition and other expenses; and (5) ROTC-related variables, including cadet enrollment, white cadet enrollment, whether the school is an ROTC host, number of commissions, and driving distance to the nearest host program.

The state-level variables are listed in Table C.3. These variables provide information on various economic characteristics as well as military members and veteran information for the state in which a school is located.

APPENDIX D

Methodology to Construct the Measures in the Reserve Officers' Training Corps Selection Evaluation Tool

This appendix describes some of the mathematics behind the desirability score and the multiple indicator model for the ROTC-SET. It is not necessary to understand the math in order to use the ROTC-SET or to modify the program, however.

Prediction of Propensity

The "Propensity" score measures the number of students who would be interested in participating in the ROTC program. To predict the number of students, we first built a logistic regression model to predict the possibility of a student being interested in the ROTC program, then multiplied the predicted possibility by the number of enrollments to get the school-level prediction.

The model is defined as

$$Ln\left(\frac{p_i}{1-p_i}\right) = \beta X_i + \varepsilon_i,$$

where p_i is the possibility of a student from school i being interested in the ROTC program, X_i and β are the school characteristics and corresponding coefficients, and ε_i is the error term. The standard errors are clustered at the school level to account for correlation within schools. We used the predicted probability of being interested in ROTC multiplied by the number of students currently enrolled at a university as the propensity score.

Estimation of Similarity

The similarity score measures the similarity of a school to ROTC host schools that produced more than an average of 15 commissions per year, based on commission data from 2009 to 2013. It is used for the "Commissions" indicator. To estimate the similarity score, we applied a logistic regression model to estimate the probability that a host school would produce more than 15 commissions per year. We then applied the model to other schools and used the predicted probability as a similarity score.

The model is defined as

$$Ln\left(\frac{p_i}{1-p_i}\right)=\beta X_i+\varepsilon_i,$$

where p_i is the possibility of a school being like a host that produced more than 15 commissions, X_i and β are the school characteristics and corresponding coefficients, and ε_i is the error term.

Prediction of Productivity

We built a two-part model to predict the number of MS 3 contracts at a school. The first part of the model is a logistic regression estimating whether a school produces any MS 3 contracts. The second part of the model is a zero truncated negative binomial model with only the schools with non-zero productions.

The first part of the model is defined as

$$Ln\left(\frac{p_i}{1-p_i}\right)=\beta X_i+\varepsilon_i,$$

where p_i is the possibility of a school producing any MS 3 contracts, X_i and β are the school characteristics and corresponding coefficients, and ε_i is the error term.

The second part is defined as

$$Log(\mu) = \beta X_i + \varepsilon_i,$$

where μ is the expected count of MS 3 contracts, X_i and β are the school characteristics and corresponding coefficients, and ε_i is the error term.

Projection of Future Enrollment

To estimate each school's enrollment in 2020, we applied an OLS regression model to each school based on enrollment data from 1987 to 2012.

The model is defined as

$$Y_t = \beta T + \varepsilon_t,$$

where Y_t denotes the enrollment in the *t*th year and T and β are school year and the corresponding coefficient. The error term ε_t is a regular first-order autoregression (AR[1]) time series with unknown variance and an autoregressive parameter. We then used the model to predict the enrollment in 2020 for each school.

Calculation of Program Retention Rates

We used maximum likelihood estimation (MLE) to calculate retention rates as empirical transition rates from MS level i to MS level $i + 1$.

Specifically, each individual (or case) contributes to the likelihood function as follows:

1. Cases that moved from MS level i to MS level $i + 1$: $Li = S(t_i)\lambda(t_i)$.
2. Cases that were censored: $L_i = S(t_i)$.

Thus, the total log likelihood function is given by

$$LogL = Log\sum_i S(t_i)\lambda(t_i)^{d_i},$$

where d_i equals 1 if the individual moves from MS i to MS $i + 1$, and 0 otherwise. The function may therefore be rewritten as

$$LogL = \sum_i d_i Log\lambda(t_i) - \Lambda(t_i).$$

We assume a constant, time-independent hazard rate of MS promotion. Hence, $\lambda(t) = \lambda$ and $\Lambda(t) = \lambda t$, so

$$LogL = \sum_i d_i Log\lambda - \lambda t_i.$$

Let D denote the total number of transitions from MS 1 to MS 2, for example, and let T denote the total exposure time (i.e., total number of cadet-years in MS 1). The above function may thus be rewritten as

$$LogL = DLog\lambda - \lambda T.$$

The MLE of the score function is therefore simply D/T, the total number of transitions divided by total exposures.

Estimated Retention Rates for Efficiency Score

We used a proportional survival model to estimate predicted retention rates at each school based on cadet, school, and state characteristics. We then calculated the "Efficiency" "Retention Score" indicator as the difference between the actual and predicted retention rates. In our model, the retention hazard is defined as the conditional probability, given that a cadet was in a program the previous year, that he/she would remain in the program in the current year, measured over the time period from fall 2008 to fall 2012.

The regression model can be written as follows:

$$\lambda(t \mid x_t, \beta) = \lambda_0(t)\phi(x_t, \beta),$$

where λ is the retention hazard at time t given a vector of cadet characteristics x_t, and λ_0 is the baseline hazard. The retention hazard is modeled as the product of the baseline hazard and a proportional multiplier ϕ, which is a function of x_t and the estimated vector of coefficients β.

Since cadet status is observed annually, we can model the transition probability continuously with the necessary adjustments for grouping data (by MS level, by cadet, by year). With grouping points denoted by t_a, $a = 1, \ldots, A$, the discrete-time hazard function is defined as

$$\lambda\left(t_a \mid x_{t_{a-1}}\right) = \Pr\left(t_{a-1} \leq T < t_a \mid T \geq t_{a-1}, x_{t_{a-1}}\right).$$

The associated discrete-time survival function is

$$S\left(t_a \mid x_{t_{a-1}}\right) = \Pr\left(T \geq t_{a-1} \mid x_{t_{a-1}}\right) = \prod_{s=1}^{a-1}\left(1 - \lambda\left(t_s \mid x_{t_{s-1}}\right)\right).$$

We included time-varying predictor variables at the cadet, school, and state levels and used a stepwise selection process to identify the set of influential variables. The statistically-significant cadet characteristics included type of scholarship, current MS level, and year of enrollment. Significant school-level attributes included school quality (i.e., whether the school is public or private and whether it is residential or nonresidential). Examples of state-level variables include the state unemployment rate, percentage of adults in the state with college degrees, and the percentage of military members in the state's population.

APPENDIX E

Regression Results for Modeling Variables Used in the Reserve Officers' Training Corps Selection Evaluation Tool

This appendix shows the regression results we used to construct variables for the ROTC-SET model: Commissions, Propensity, Potential Productivity, and Retention Score. See Chapter Three for a discussion of these variables. For the origin of the data we used to construct those variables, see Appendix C; for the methodology behind the creation of these variables, see Appendix D.

Tables E.1 through E.5 show how much different variables contributed to the final, constructed variables. For instance, Table E.1 shows the regression results for the "Commissions" variable, or the similarity of schools in the ROTC-SET to existing schools with ROTC programs that produce 15 or more commissions per year. Tables E.2 and E.5 have the same format. Tables E.3 and E.4, for "Potential Productivity," are somewhat different because "Potential Productivity" is a two-step model: see the explanation of that model in Appendix D. Additionally, for all of these tables, the reader should keep in mind that over a sufficient period of time there will be new data. At that point it will be preferable to run new regression models using the new data in order to generate new coefficients, rather than to continue to use the coefficients shown below. There are two options for running the new models. The first is to just reestimate the same models. The second is to repeat the stepwise process for determining which variables to include in the models as well as reestimating the coefficients.

We can take two approaches for testing the goodness of fit for our regression models. One is to compare across models with different sets of variables, interactions, and other model specifications. The Akaike

Table E.1
Logistic Regression Results for the "Commissions" Variable Indicating the Probability That a School Will Produce at Least 15 Commissions

Variable	Coefficient	Standard Error
Enrollment (unit: 1,000)	0.370***	0.045
Enrollment squared	–0.005***	0.001
Total yearly expense (tuition, room, and board; unit: $1,000)	–0.065	0.047
Total yearly expense squared (unit: $1,000)	0.001*	0.001
State median household income (unit: $1,000)	–0.023	0.013
Acceptance rate	0.019**	0.007
Graduation total	0.021*	0.010
Percentage of full-time faculty	0.020**	0.008
Percentage of male students	0.051***	0.010
Percentage of military members in the state	0.969	0.547
Percentage of veterans in the county within a one-hour driving distance	0.169	0.052
Constant	–10.400***	1.469

NOTE: Significance levels are *** = 0.001, ** = 0.01, and * = 0.05.

information criterion (AIC) and the Bayesian information criterion (BIC) are widely-used methods for comparing models with different specifications. These methods are straightforward to implement and useful for excluding irrelevant variables because they penalize for increasing the number of independent variables. After selecting a list of potential independent variables, identifying the functional form for these variables, and applying the forward and backward selection processes, we ended up with a range of candidate models. We used the AIC and BIC (in addition to the Pearson and Hosmer–Lemeshow tests or, alternatively, the specification link test) to identify the best-performing models. The AIC and BIC results for these models were as good as or better than those of all other candidate models. Of the four applicable models, three pass both the Pearson and Hosmer–Lemeshow

Table E.2
Logistic Regression Results for the "Propensity" Variable Indicating the Probability of a Student Being Interested in the ROTC Program

Variable	Coefficient	Standard Error
Total yearly expense (tuition, room, and board; unit: $1,000)	−0.033	0.017
Total yearly expense squared (unit: $1,000)	0.001*	0.000
State median household income (unit: $1,000)	0.019*	0.009
Percentage of African American students	0.000	0.001
Percentage of Hispanic students	0.005**	0.002
Percentage of male students	0.014***	0.003
Diversity index	−0.441**	0.152
Accession rate	−0.160*	0.077
State unemployment rate	0.025	0.046
Percentage of adults in the state with college degrees	−0.057***	0.012
Number of veterans per 1,000 state population	0.004	0.003
Northeast Region	0.080	0.111
Midwest Region	−0.173*	0.085
West Region	0.200*	0.080
Constant	−0.538	0.568

NOTE: Significance levels are *** = 0.001, ** = 0.01, and * = 0.05.

tests. The "Retention Score" model did not pass the tests, but it was the best possible model specification given the data and variables we had. Also, note that the Pearson and Hosmer–Lemeshow tests are not applicable to the zero truncated negative model that was used for the second stage of the "Potential Productivity" model. So instead, we used the specification link test, which the model did pass.

Table E.3
First Part of Hurdle Regression Results for Potential Productivity: Whether a School Will Have Any MS 3 Contracts

Variable	Coefficient	Standard Error
Log(enrollment) (unit: 1,000)	–1.496***	0.107
Log(total yearly expense) (unit: $1,000)	0.873**	0.298
Public school	1.404***	0.290
SAT or ACT 75th percentile (2nd quartile)	–0.293	0.194
SAT or ACT 75th percentile (3rd quartile)	–0.331	0.225
SAT or ACT 75th percentile (4th quartile)	–0.316	0.271
SAT or ACT 75th percentile (missing)	–0.922**	0.294
Acceptance rate	–0.007	0.004
Graduation rate	–0.016*	0.007
Appropriations per postsecondary student	0.132**	0.046
Percentage of full-time faculty	0.012**	0.004
Percentage of African American students	–0.007	0.004
Percentage of Hispanic students	0.019***	0.005
Percentage of male students	–0.014**	0.006
Percentage of military members in the state	–0.805	0.462
Northeast Region	0.492*	0.237
Midwest Region	0.650**	0.214
West Region	0.023	0.254
Constant	–2.043	1.154

NOTE: Significance levels are *** = 0.001, ** = 0.01, and * = 0.05. The SAT or ACT 75th percentile quartiles are dummy variables representing the quartile in the national distribution of SAT or ACT scores of the school's 75th percentile score.

Table E.4
Hurdle Regression Results for Potential Productivity: Number of MS 3 Contracts

Variable	Incidence Rate Ratio	Standard Error
Log(enrollment) (unit: 1,000)	2.208***	0.100
State median household income (unit: $1,000)	0.984*	0.007
Primarily-resident school	1.231	0.136
SAT or ACT 75th percentile (2nd quartile)	1.017	0.119
SAT or ACT 75th percentile (3rd quartile)	1.253	0.163
SAT or ACT 75th percentile (4th quartile)	0.862	0.141
SAT or ACT 75th percentile (missing)	1.055	0.173
Graduation rate	1.011**	0.004
Percentage of full-time faculty	1.007**	0.002
Percentage of instructors with doctorate or terminal degrees	0.998	0.001
Percentage of students in physical science and engineering majors	0.991	0.005
Percentage of male students	1.045***	0.004
Diversity index	0.512**	0.099
Percentage of adults in the state with college degrees	1.022	0.015
Percentage of veterans in the county within one hour's driving distance	1.110***	0.019
Northeast Region	0.550***	0.070
Midwest Region	0.734**	0.079
West Region	0.951	0.133
Constant	0.107***	0.065

NOTE: Significance levels are *** = 0.001, ** = 0.01, and * = 0.05. The SAT or ACT 75th percentile quartiles are dummy variables representing the quartile in the national distribution of SAT or ACT scores of the school's 75th percentile score.

Table E.5
Logistic Regression Results for Retention Score Predicting Whether a Cadet Will Remain in the ROTC Program

Variable	Coefficient	Standard Error
Log(enrollment) (unit: 1,000)	–0.038	0.020
Log(total yearly expense) (unit: $1,000)	–0.399***	0.037
Type of scholarship (baseline: no scholarship)		
Two year	–0.953***	0.044
Three year	–1.205***	0.047
Four year	–1.393***	0.026
Graduate	–1.470***	0.271
Public school	–0.174 ***	0.050
Primarily-resident school	0.105 ***	0.028
SAT or ACT 75th percentile (baseline: 1st quartile)		
2nd quartile	0.109**	0.040
3rd quartile	–0.051	0.042
4th quartile	–0.142**	0.048
Missing	0.152*	0.068
Acceptance rate	0.002**	0.001
Appropriations per postsecondary student	–0.035***	0.007
Percentage of full-time faculty	0.004***	0.001
Percentage of instructors with doctorate or terminal degrees	0.001**	0.000
Percentage of African American students	0.006***	0.001
Percentage of Hispanic students	0.001	0.001
Percentage of male students	0.002*	0.001
Accession rate	0.046	0.033
State unemployment rate	0.067***	0.007
Percentage of adults in the state with college degrees	–0.005	0.003

Table E.5—Continued

Variable	Coefficient	Standard Error
Percentage of military members in the state	0.148*	0.064
Percentage of the state population within one hour's driving distance who are veterans	–0.010	0.006
MS level (baseline: MS 1)		
2	–0.770***	0.027
3	–2.112***	0.030
4	–3.330***	0.039
5	–3.762***	0.231
6	–3.037***	0.187
7	–3.127***	0.081
Year of enrollment (baseline: 2002)		
2003	–0.205***	0.042
2004	–0.448***	0.042
2005	–0.664***	0.042
2006	–0.806***	0.041
2007	–1.522***	0.043
2008	–2.858***	0.050
2009	–0.106*	0.051
2010	0.429***	0.064
Constant	3.167 ***	0.290

NOTE: Significance levels are *** = 0.001, ** = 0.01, and * = 0.05. Type of scholarship is a cadet's scholarship type. MS level is a cadet's year of ROTC. Year of enrollment is the year of a cadet's enrollment in ROTC.

References

Career Satisfaction Program, "Order of Merit Score Calculations Briefing Slides," undated. As of May 10, 2016:
http://www.career-satisfaction.army.mil/rotc_order_of_merit.html

DoDI 1215.08—*See* Under Secretary of Defense for Personnel and Readiness, 2006.

GAO—*See* U.S. Government Accountability Office.

Indiana University Center for Postsecondary Research, *The Carnegie Classification of Institutions of Higher Education*, 2005 ed., Bloomington, Ind., undated.

Public Law 112-239, National Defense Authorization Act for Fiscal Year 2013, January 2, 2013. As of May 10, 2016:
https://www.gpo.gov/fdsys/pkg/PLAW-112publ239/pdf/PLAW-112publ239.pdf

R Foundation, "The R Project for Statistical Computing," undated. As of May 12, 2016:
https://www.r-project.org/

RStudio, "Download RStudio," undated. As of May 12, 2016:
https://www.rstudio.com/products/rstudio/download/

Secretary of the Army, *Army Senior Reserve Officers' Training Corps (SROTC) Annual Program Review*, 2014.

Under Secretary of Defense for Personnel and Readiness, *Senior Reserve Officers' Training Corps (ROTC) Programs*, Washington, D.C., Department of Defense Instruction 1215.08, June 26, 2006. As of May 9, 2016:
http://www.dtic.mil/whs/directives/corres/pdf/121508p.pdf

U.S. Government Accountability Office, *Military Personnel: Actions Needed to Improve Evaluation and Oversight of Reserve Officers' Training Corps Programs*, Washington, D.C., GAO-14-93, November 13, 2013. As of May 9, 2016:
http://www.gao.gov/products/GAO-14-93